C000265125

Reflections from a Marriage

The Authors

Roger and Susan Sawtell met via the Iona Community and were married in 1957, aged 30 and 25. Roger was Works Director of Spear & Jackson, steel and tool makers in Sheffield, and Susan was working at Sheffield Children's Hospital as an Occupational Therapist. Ten years later, now with four small children, Roger resigned from his job and they made a family sabbatical journey overland to Jerusalem and stayed on a kibbutz in Galilee, returning via the Taizé community in France with which they had been involved since 1958.

On reaching the UK again in 1968 they moved to Northampton to enable Roger to develop Trylon Ltd, an employee-owned co-operative business making glassfibre canoes. When the children were all school age, Susan returned to occupational therapy in child development, and later with older people. In 1980, Roger, now a co-operative entrepreneur, was founding member of another employee-owned business, Daily Bread Co-operative in Northampton. Since 1984 they have lived in a residential ecumenical Christian community, The Neighbours Community, which occupies five adjoining terrace houses. Susan has been attending Northampton Quaker Meeting since 1986 and Roger is an interdenominational Christian. Since retirement, they have been involved with people recovering from mental illness, the spirituality of ageing, peace and justice issues, and their eight grandchildren.

Reflections
from a Long Marriage

Roger and Susan Sawtell

Swarthmore Lecture 2006

QUAKERbooks

First published May 2006

Quaker Books, Friends House, 173 Euston Road,
London NW1 2BJ

www.quaker.org.uk

All rights reserved. No part of this book may
be reproduced or transmitted in any form or by
any means, electronic or mechanical, including
photocopy, without permission in writing from
Quaker Books.

ISBN 0 85245 394 9

© Roger and Susan Sawtell 2006. The moral
rights of Roger and Susan Sawtell as authors of
this work are asserted in accordance with the
Copyright, Designs and Patents Act 1988.

Text design Golden Cockerel Press Ltd, London

Cover design Hoop Associates
Cover image Manoj Shah (Getty Images)

For copyright reasons this edition is not for sale in
Egypt or Israel.

Further copyright statements appear under
"Acknowledgements", page 8.

Printed and bound in Great Britain
by Biddles Ltd, King's Lynn, Norfolk

The Swarthmore Lecture

The Swarthmore Lectureship was established by the Woodbrooke Extension Committee at a meeting held 9 December 1907: the minute of the Committee providing for an "annual lecture on some subject relating to the message and work of the Society of Friends". The name Swarthmore was chosen in memory of the home of Margaret Fox, which was always open to the earnest seeker after Truth, and from which loving words of sympathy and substantial material help were sent to fellow workers.

The Lectureship continues to be under the care of Woodbrooke Quaker Study Centre trustees, and is a significant part of the education work undertaken at and from Woodbrooke.

The lectureship has a twofold purpose: first, to interpret to the members of the Society of Friends their message and mission; and second, to bring before the public the spirit, aims and fundamental principles of Friends. The lecturers alone are responsible for any opinions expressed.

The lectureship provides both for the publication of a book and for the delivery of a lecture, the latter usually at the time of Britain Yearly Meeting of the Society of Friends. A lecture related to the present book was delivered at Yearly Meeting in London on the evening of 27 May 2006.

The Swarthmore Lecture Committee can be contacted via the Clerk, c/o Woodbrooke Quaker Study Centre, 1046 Bristol Road, Selly Oak, Birmingham B29 6LJ.

A word of explanation

"When I use a word", Humpty Dumpty said . . . "it means
just what I choose it to mean – neither more nor less".

Lewis Carroll, *Through the Looking Glass*

Throughout this book we use the word "marriage", and the phrase "a
married couple", in an inclusive sense. Of course "a married couple"
denotes those legally married in church, registry office or elsewhere
but we have chosen to give it a wider meaning to include all people,
of different sex or same sex, who are committed to each other in
a **lifelong loving relationship**, some of whom may not legally be
married.

Cartoon p.9 by Ray Liberty

"Marriage" p.15 reproduced with permission © Quaker Tapestry
Scheme, Friends Meeting House, Stramongate, Kendal, Cumbria
LA9 4BH. www.quaker-tapestry.co.uk

Sketches pp.17, 37, 43, 62, 87, 94, 98, 100 by Jane Roberts

Drawing of the Neighbours Community p.29 by Pam Frier

Drawing p.37 by Martin Reardon, published in the newsletter
of the Association of Interchurch Families, reproduced by
permission of the artist's widow

Wedding photograph p.42 by John & Dorothy Kirkman, Sutton
Coldfield

"Why Marriage?" p.50–51 © Posy Simmonds reprinted by
permission of PFD on behalf of Posy Simmonds

Mural p.103 by Mary Williams, © Daily Bread Co-operative

Extract from *The Original Revolution* by John Howard Yoder.
Copyright 1971, 1977, 2003 by Herald Press, Scottdale, PA 15683.
Used by permission.

Extract from *A Patchwork Planet* by Anne Tyler. reprinted by
permission of The Random House Group. Published by Chatto &
Windus, (UK and Commonwealth except Canada); and by Alfred
A. Knopf for USA, Canada and remaining territories.

Acknowledgements

We are grateful to the Swarthmore Lecture Committee of the Religious Society of Friends for their invitation to write this book. Whether or not we have something useful to communicate is for you, the reader, to judge. Suffice to say that it has been a useful discipline for us to get our lifetime thoughts and conclusions into some sort of order, and on paper rather than just swirling around in our heads.

It is impossible to write at first hand about a long marriage without being old and as we get older we see the failures and disappointments of our friends and colleagues and so we grow more cautious and look more carefully for the potholes in the path ahead. There is also a mental slowing-down process and we find it less demanding to stay with well-known routines rather than trying new paths. We lose the ability to see the promised land and only see the mountain range which obscures it. We take the road more travelled and become more resistant to the less travelled way. To counteract these tendencies of age we have concentrated our writing on the upside-down parts of our lives, which took place between the ages of forty and seventy. Most of the changes in the world, particularly the positive ones, are initiated by people under seventy and so we write in hope to the younger half of the Society, knowing that no one path is right for everyone but knowing also that there is much latent talent among Friends for living the testimonies at home and at work.

Our mentors, appointed by the Swarthmore Lecture Committee, encouraged us to be bold in our writing and we have heeded their advice. Consequently, some of what follows may be contentious and some, coming from a partnership which is only half Quaker, may be considered downright presumptuous especially to weighty Friends of a conservative disposition. Needless to say, we take total responsibility for what we have written and we record our grateful thanks to our liaison friends, Geoffrey Carnall and Julia Gordon, and to the numerous Friends and friends who have helped us. We thank Pam Lunn at Woodbrooke, who has been endlessly supportive, Rachel Howell at St Francis House, Oxford, who has patiently helped us to get the writing on to the screen without getting lost in the depths of the computer, Jane Roberts who has contributed the drawings, and Peter Daniels and his colleagues at Friends House.

Written with Friends in mind, our text is peppered with references to that wonderful book, *Quaker Faith & Practice*, which deserves a wider circulation among faith communities of all descriptions. From discussions during the writing, it is apparent that our book will be read by numerous non-Quakers who will not be familiar with the meaning attached to words such as "convincement" or "prevented", or mysterious phrases like "that name would not have occurred to me". Therefore we have tried to avoid Quaker jargon and abbreviations or to explain them where unavoidable. We hope that Friends will not find this too tedious and will accept it as outreach.

Roger and Susan Sawtell,
Northampton, December 2005

Publisher's note:
References to books quoted appear in brackets with the author's name or short title under which full details can be found in the book list at the back.

Contents

1 Introduction

As well as their outward and visible work for justice and peace there was a time when Quakers were also recognised by the general public for their distinctive clothes in subdued colours and for an alternative lifestyle, both at home and at work. Now, in 2006, the public witness remains strong but the contents of Friends' clothes cupboards, larders or bathroom shelves are unlikely to differ much from those of the secular majority. Our own shelves are no different but, looking back on nearly fifty years of marriage we realise, somewhat to our own surprise, that we have lived a different lifestyle to most of those around us and that our experience may have relevance for the 21st century. Furthermore, as a "mixed marriage" of a Quaker to a non-Quaker, it seems to us that some of the insights of the Religious Society of Friends may now be appropriate to organisations well beyond the Meeting House. For example, the decision-making process developed by Quakers over many years is particularly relevant to the kind of inter-denominational residential community in which we have lived for nearly half our married life and also relevant to employee-owned businesses such as Daily Bread Co-operative which, since its inception in 1976, has been part of our life together. As a further example, most "communities of households", including the one we describe hereafter, have a concern for simplicity rather than complexity and for frugality rather than the extravagance and waste that is now commonplace in the rich society in which we find ourselves.

Both of us became active Christians in our student years, before we met each other; Susan via the Iona Community* and Roger via an evangelical student mission. All our married life we have been trying to discover, in practical ways, what it means to keep the faith two thousand years after Jesus. Neither of us has felt called to be a minister

*An ecumenical Christian community founded in 1938 by George MacLeod, gathered round the rebuilding of the ancient monastic buildings on the island of Iona off the west coast of Scotland.

of religion nor have we been called to the monastic life, hardly an option for married couples, although we have benefited from close association with monasteries in several different parts of the world. However, looking for guidance in our reading of the Bible particularly to the time of Jesus' ministry and the small groups of his followers during the subsequent sixty years during which the Gospels were written, we have felt ourselves inexorably drawn towards counter-cultural groups.

Friends will understand this because they have usually assumed that their values and testimonies would lead them towards a lifestyle significantly different from the surrounding culture. Janey O'Shea writes:

> In the topsy-turvy world of the Way of God as taught by Jesus, familiar categories turn upside down, people with contagious diseases are touched and healed; a woman who prefers intellectual discussion to housework is highly valued; the unemployed get a day's wage for a few hours' work; a prostitute is held up as a good example to a religious leader; the good seats at a state banquet go to the street people . . . the charism of early Friends was their gift to live at home in the upside down world of God's reign (O'Shea 1993 p.62).

Thus we have been more anxious when our lifestyle refuses to be upside down than the times when we have been led to be counter-cultural.

We have a problem in tackling this writing project. We are asked to write experientially rather than academically or theoretically. What can we say from our own direct experience of a long marriage? Well, for a start we can say that our marriage has survived during a period when separation and divorce have become increasingly frequent. If it were not so, we would not be writing.

In 1957, the year of our marriage, over 400,000 couples got married in the UK but by 2001 this figure had diminished by 28% to 286,000. The corresponding figures for divorce over this same period increased by 86%, from 80,000 to 157,000. One or two of our long-married friends even feel they need to apologise for remaining married when those around them may be distressed or embittered by their

Quaker marriage (reproduced with permission © Quaker tapestry Scheme)

"failure" to hold their marriages together, particularly those married with the beautiful Quaker wording:

> Friends, I take this my friend N. to be my wife, promising, with God's help, to be unto her a loving and faithful husband, so long as we both on earth shall live (*Quaker Faith & Practice* 16.36).*

Friends do not take such promises lightly and the testimony to truth and integrity makes them all the more significant.

Our problem is how to write in such a way that our experience does not seem pretentious. All we can say is that we are aware of the

---

*The sentence quoted is one of several allowable variations in the wording of the Quaker marriage declaration set out in 16.36. Some wedding ceremonies, not Quaker ones, have a wide variety of promises, conditional clauses, etc. but *QFP* 16.36 includes a rather threatening sentence – "No other changes to the wording may be made".

pitfalls of marriage and have experienced one or two, but we have enjoyed being married and we still do enjoy it. We have no personal experience of separation or of divorce and do not propose to write at length about them, especially as there is already a large body of literature on the subject. On the other hand, little has been written on the positive aspects of contemporary marriage and it is not fashionable to do so. We ask the forbearance of readers if we appear to make the grass too green on our side of the fence as we have no wish to cause feelings of guilt or failure among those whose marriages have not lasted, sometimes for reasons totally beyond their control.

Some books written by two people, rather than one author, appear disjointed and this may be particularly apparent in this book because we have different ways of looking at the world around us. This appears for instance on the "Myers-Briggs Type Indicator" (see Myers 1980), where the answers are formulated to classify individual personality under four headings – extrovert/introvert (E/I); sensing/intuition (N/S); thinking/feeling (T/F); judging/perceiving (J/P): Susan usually comes out as INFP and Roger as ISTJ. We have the I in common but we differ in each of the other three headings. If our writing has any value it may be because it shows how the same circumstances, a long marriage, can be seen in significantly different ways by the two people most closely involved in it. Some readers may respond to one view and some to the other. Nevertheless, during this writing we have become aware of the synergy of a lifelong loving relationship. The energy of two people in a long marriage is greater than the sum of the energy of the same two people not in such a relationship.

"The Religious Society of Friends is rooted in Christianity and has always found inspiration in the life and teaching of Jesus" (*QFP* 1.02 "Advices and Queries" no.4). A group of highly respected Bible scholars who spent years searching for the authentic words of Jesus* came to the conclusion that his phrases were more everyday and

---

* See Funk *et al*, *The Five Gospels*, 1997. The Bible quotations throughout this book are either from this "colloquial translation" (abbreviated to *TFG*), or from the New Revised Standard Version (NRSV; OUP 1989), generally agreed by scholars to be the most accurate of the modern translations, although for us, Bible readers and listeners for many years, it does not have the familiarity nor the poetic language of the Authorised Version.

colloquial than is sometimes gathered from reading the Authorised Version or the contemporary translations into modern English. Jesus would have spoken as a carpenter, not as an academic. A crowd gathered to listen to him would have been more like an early Quaker outdoor meeting than a lecture room, and the people a diverse group rather than students with notebooks or church people in pews. Correspondingly, in writing this book, we understand that we are addressing a very varied readership which will include carpenters and professors, pensioners and students.

John Howard Yoder writes, "In other societies and cultures, people are plagued by anxiety, guilt, fear of judgment. In this context the good news is stated in terms of forgiveness, acceptance by God and acceptance by other [people]. . . . But for Jesus in his time, and for increasing numbers of us in our time, the basic human problem is seen in less individualistic terms. The priority agenda for Jesus and for many of us, is not mortality or anxiety, but unrighteousness, injustice. The need is not for consolation or acceptance but for a new order in which [people] may live together in love" (Yoder 1971).

We are not academics nor theologians, so what follows is not the result of scholarly research. We write only out of our direct experience of a long marriage and an unusual lifestyle, some faltering steps towards a new order, so our language may have something in common with Jesus' colloquialism. In his footsteps, we offer this book with all the love and understanding we can muster.

2 Our Spiritual Journeys

¶ Roger writes . . .

Childhood

My parents were both "Sheffield people" and I was born there as were
my elder brother and my younger sister. Although a major city with
a population of half a million, Sheffield in the 1930s was remarkably
self-contained and even parochial. Steel was dominant and my father
worked in the industry all his life, as had my maternal grandfather
although the latter seems to have spent a good deal of his time and
money on entertaining "chorus girls" visiting the local theatre. He
was an embarrassment to my mother and frittered away whatever
money came into his possession. Neither of my parents inherited
any money from their parents and with three children to bring up
they had to be very careful about spending. Susan says we must
have lived in "genteel poverty" but I have no recollection of being
materially deprived. We were a happy family. My father was high-
principled but not imaginative, my mother was tender and loving; he
thought the world of her and she sighed from time to time but was
obedient and "no trouble". To the three of us she was incomparable.
My parents were both committed and active members of the Church
of England and we were brought up in that tradition and sat through
countless long forgotten services, mostly matins in the village church.
The words of the Book of Common Prayer are deeply embedded in my
subconscious.

My mother read the Bible to us with love for the words and
conviction in her voice. Nearly all of it passed straight over my head
but some of the stories were exciting and I wondered if the walls of our
house would fall down if, like Joshua, I marched round long enough
blowing a tin trumpet. They did not fall and I gained no faith. After
she died, I retrieved her Bible and learned that she read the New
Testament every day, round and round every five years and pencilled
the dates into the margin. Clearly this was a major influence in her
life and although I did not receive the charism of faith until years
afterwards, I am most grateful for this biblical grounding which has

stayed with me all my life. Time and again I recollect the wonderful language of the Authorised Version, full of memorable phrases and beautiful poetry.

In the tradition of the middle classes, I was sent away to school, aged eight, to Arnold House in North Wales where Evelyn Waugh had been, briefly, on the staff some years earlier. The Bishop of Chester, Geoffrey Fisher, sent his sons there so, as good Anglicans, my parents thought it would be a respectable Christian establishment. What they apparently did not know, and neither did the Bishop, who subsequently became Archbishop of Canterbury, was that the owner and headmaster of the school, a born salesman but not a born-again Christian, was a charlatan. In due course his Rolls Royce with built-in cocktail cabinet disappeared and he went to prison for financial fraud or for sexually molesting small boys or possibly both. We attended chapel every day but the words still failed to register with me and cricket was a much more important religion than Christianity. The only hymn I could play on the hideous chapel harmonium was "Glory Be To Jesus", which must be the simplest tune in the book, so the school was subjected to it week after week.

I learned that "to turn the other cheek" means to refuse to be humiliated. It is active not passive. My friend Mudford was slighted by an authoritarian teacher and, braver than me, plotted revenge by ordering a hundred cheese waffles in Mr Banks's name and arranging for them to be delivered during Latin.

"There's a package for you, sir," said Mudford, carrying in a huge carton, "and the carrier wants to be paid straight away."

"I think it will be the new Latin primers, give him the money," said Mr Banks.

In due course at the end of the lesson, he opened the carton. "Oh sir," cried Mudford, "it's cheese waffles. How kind of you, sir."

Exit furious Latin teacher, seriously out of pocket.

All this and much more at this extraordinary school was more exciting than the Gospel and I remained a passive churchgoer until, to my surprise, I underwent a conversion experience at a mission at Great St Mary's, Cambridge. Yes, truly converted, changed, in that I became convinced of the truth of the Jesus story and its significance for my life. Jesus is the human embodiment of God, forgiveness and reconciliation are for real, change is possible, love is the driving force, good will eventually overcome evil. For me it was a revelation which has stayed with me ever since. Thereafter, as a graduate engineering apprentice in Rugby, I joined an evangelical church, taught very badly in Sunday school, made some lifelong friends but few converts. I did however develop some kind of prayer discipline which, much later, was transformed into corporate morning prayers when we started The Neighbours Community.

Sheffield

My parents were glad to hear of my conversion although such matters were seldom discussed at home, faith being taken for granted. They had been through a hard time as my father had lost his job and had been out of work for a year before finding work in 1938 as manager of the Light Departments at Samuel Fox, a huge steelworks outside Sheffield. At Fox's he supported the early development of the Sheffield Industrial Mission (SIM), a pioneering attempt to engage with the steel industry, inspired by the Bishop of Sheffield, Leslie Hunter. My father negotiated the crucial access to the works for Ted Wickham, the leader of SIM, and this remarkable project was often discussed at home when I returned to Sheffield in 1950 to work at Spear & Jackson, a medium-sized old-established company making special steels and woodworking tools. My father retired and Ted was quick to grab hold of me and involve me in the web of discussion groups, communion services and Bible study which made up the Industrial Mission. My evangelical fervour had been rather tentative and it then diminished because the SIM was concerned with the social Gospel rather than getting steelworkers into church; I was happy with this emphasis and concerned to seek for justice in the organisation of industrial work. Susan claims that I remain a "closet evangelical".

I enjoyed my work at Spear & Jackson and stayed for sixteen years. I soon became interested more in people than engineering technology and climbed the management ladder as fast as I could. The hours were long and the holidays short but I did not complain, being ambitious and the first graduate ever employed by the company which was founded in 1760. We made high-quality products and it gave me satisfaction to see them crated-up and despatched all over the world.

In the 1950s German industry was still recovering from the devastation of the Second World War, developing countries did not yet have sophisticated steel industries, so our only trade rivals were Sweden and the USA. Sales were easy to come by and increasing production was the problem, my particular concern as an aspiring manager of the saw department. I went to visit our competitor, Disston, in Philadelphia south of New York, and, being naive and cheeky, asked them to show me round their works because I wanted to see if they had high production machines that we could copy. Their production director met me at the station, stood me a fine lunch, drove me round the perimeter track of their huge factory in his Cadillac and took me back to the station, saying, "There you are, Mr Sawtell, I've shown you round. Goodbye." I never set foot inside the factory.

I learned a great deal from the works people in Sheffield, many of them highly skilled manual workers, loyal to the company and totally ignored when decisions were made. The directors were partly the descendants of the Jackson family, rather tired but determined to maintain the prosperity of the company, partly because it was tradition to be "a good employer" in a rather paternalistic manner and partly because there was a crowd of absentee family shareholders, mostly widows, who never came near the works but depended on the dividends.

When I was promoted to works manager, I made a point of visiting the night shift now and again. My predecessor had never done so. One night I found a lathe operator sound asleep beside his machine so I woke him up. He said he had finished his "quota" and I told him there were no quotas, production must be maximised, and I sent him home without pay. Exactly a year later, when passing his machine during tea break, he called me over and gave me a tin cup of tea from his can, saying that this was our anniversary and we should celebrate it. No hard feelings. I began to realise that we, the management, were both ignoring and exploiting our skilled workers who were willing to work in partnership with management and share their knowledge of the production processes on which the success of the company had rested for two centuries. I determined to do something about it but had no idea what to do. The gift of a clock and an exiguous pension after forty years service seemed not only inadequate but shameful.

Then I was made a director, introduced an employee shareholding scheme but was not at all satisfied that I was addressing the heart of the matter. The Industrial Mission chaplains needed to be on good terms with both management and unions and so they tended to avoid talk of structural change but the more they led me to study the social Gospel theologians, the more convinced I became that there was need for a different kind of ownership and decision-making.

During these Sheffield years until 1957, I lived a bachelor life, playing squash and cricket, going to decorous parties on the edge of the Sheffield social scene but never quite happy with it, having a succession of second-hand cars but no girl friends worthy of that description, only partners at occasional dances. Sailing was a holiday to look forward to and when cruising in Scotland we anchored off Iona, explored the island, and met George MacLeod, the charismatic leader of the Iona Community. "Ha!" he said, "You Anglicans are obsessed with the Apostolic Succession." This mystified us because, although we knew a good deal about sailing, we were totally unaware of the sensitivities of the Church of Scotland about bishops and stuff. However, we caught a glimpse of his vision and my brother, architect and matchmaker, returned later in the summer, to be a volunteer guide at Iona Abbey. From the island, he phoned me to say he had met three young women who were living in Sheffield and one of them was sure to be a suitable wife for me. Two were occupational therapists. I tried one who was nice but a bit ditsy and then another with dark hair and a lovely wide smile. I was late twenties and do not remember that I was specifically looking for a wife, who might interfere with work or squash, but this was too good a chance to miss. We went to the movies and held hands, I think.

When Susan and her friends returned from Iona, they had also become involved with the Sheffield Industrial Mission and Ted Wickham was our friend and subsequently married us. We were both much influenced by this remarkable mission experience in which we were expected to know the writing of theologians like Tillich, Bonhoeffer and William Temple. These years were our grounding in left-leaning Christian socialism and, although the Mission faded away under a new bishop, the teaching has stayed with both of us to this day and led us along paths which would have surprised our parents. I had been brought up in a Conservative-voting household but shocked my father by joining the Liberal Party, and later the Labour Party for many years. I wanted to see change in industry and the Liberals were promoting it at that time. Susan's grandfather had been a solicitor in Derby and a Labour Councillor. He took on industrial injury claims for the National Union of Railwaymen and was made a Freeman of Derby with an amazing Crown Derby casket to contain the scroll. He was offered a knighthood but refused because he did not approve of the honours system. I say that his legacy remains in the characters of his two granddaughters.

Susan's father continued this political concern as a successful barrister and later became a judge. He was a National Labour MP from 1931 to 1935 and still holds the record for the smallest majority in Parliamentary history, just two votes after several recounts. He worked with J.H. Thomas, prominent trade unionist and cabinet minister under Ramsay MacDonald and when Susan was born in 1932, Jimmy Thomas became her godfather. So she brought with her to our growing friendship a strong concern for social justice which chimed with my state of mind. What more could one want of a girl friend?

My friend Derek and I had a share in a four-berth yacht, based in Cornwall, and we paid Susan and Derek's friend, Mary, the ultimate compliment of inviting them to come sailing with us to the Scilly Isles. There was to be no sharing of bunks of course, this was 1955, so Derek and I had the main cabin and the girls had to make do with the fo'castle which was a lot more cramped. On the way back to Falmouth we ran into a severe gale off Lands End, in which several other yachts sank and crews were drowned. All four of us were reduced by sea sickness to lying on the cabin floor with the boat hove-to. What humiliation. In the middle of this stormy night, miles from land, I crawled out on to the heaving deck to empty my heaving stomach, and saw a huge black shape off our starboard bow, towering over our small yacht. It was a freighter moving up channel, her propeller thrashing half out of the water as she crested each huge wave. But for the grace of God . . . we could have been run down and drowned without trace as we were too sick to keep a lookout and small boats do not always show up on the radar screen of a merchant ship in bad weather. We staggered into Falmouth, wet and dispirited.

Susan survived this test and back in Yorkshire on comparatively dry land, we walked on the moors and talked about life and social justice. I was no great lover but was regarded by Sheffield matrons as "quite a catch" as a director of a well-known steel firm and a Freeman of the Cutlers' Company, the livery company which dominated the city. I proposed to her somewhere above Derwent reservoir. She might have said to herself, "how can I even think of marrying this slightly smug, judgmental man with his crackpot ideas about industrial democracy which may lead to financial ruin?", but in the event, alleluia!, she said yes and we decided we would live happily ever after. Love would find a way. Susan's recollections of our courting may be different.

℘ *Susan writes . . .*

But, take heart, just because you wonder if you and your partner have been at the same event, lived the same life, it does not mean that only one view of that life is the valid one. Each view can inform the other if only we can learn to hear what the other is saying. "Glass half empty, glass half full" can create a full glass, flowing over, giving life. Roger is out there telling it all and I am trying to gear-up the energy to say something. He needs curbing and I need encouraging but if it were left to me little would be achieved, although we might all be marginally more comfortable. If it were left to him the world would be a better place but we would all be exhausted!

When I was a toddler my mother could sit me on the lawn surrounded by the hose-pipe and there I would stay. The hose-pipe was apparently insurmountable! Life also seemed insurmountable and I crept along, hoping it would go away and occasionally trying to go away from it. I once escaped down the roof of my dormitory but couldn't think what to do with this apparent freedom and crept back again. My sister was the adventurous one; I kept quiet but enjoyed the intellectual challenge of my father's social concerns and political involvement. The conversations at meals about the issues of the day ill-prepared me for the social life of Oxford, where I was at college training to be an occupational therapist. I was glad to find a hiding place in the company of other people concerned with the social Gospel in the Presbyterian Church, which had strong links, through its minister, with the Iona Community. I did not realise that this was my first step towards Roger!

¶ *Roger writes . . .*

Susan joined the Presbyterian Church when she came to work in Sheffield in 1954. However, my links with Iona and with the Sheffield Industrial Mission caused me to become only a marginal member of a parish congregation in Sheffield. When we married in 1957, we thought it important to go to one church rather than two so we became members of the parish church in Broomhill, Sheffield, where we lived until 1968. The vicar was Michael Adie, who supported my close involvement with industrial mission and did not expect to see much of me at parish events. Susan, with the children, was a more regular attender. This somewhat uncertain link with the established church is exemplified by the children's baptisms, each at a different place, Ruth at a daughter church, Mary at an Industrial Mission eucharist at Sheffield Cathedral, Rebecca in the church hall and Peter at our parish church.

During the 1960s we made several visits to the monastic community of Taizé in central France, dedicated to Christian unity and to working with "the poorest of the poor". Two of the Brothers came to Sheffield and became our friends; Frère Jan, a qualified child psychologist, worked as a hospital porter and Frère Roland as a steelworks labourer at Spear & Jackson, totally demanding physically but not intellectually. We were moved by their humility and by the depth of Taizé worship, periods of silence interspersed by singing the repetitive chants that later became known all over the world. Taizé was an influence on both of us to make the life-changing decision to leave Sheffield in 1968 and move to Northampton for me to take up an opportunity to initiate an employee-owned co-operative business, Trylon, making fibreglass canoes.

Northampton

¶ *Susan writes . . .*

We were the first of our friendship group to move from Sheffield. We had only one contact in Northampton, a former Industrial Mission chaplain and his family. We could hardly have chosen a place of greater contrast, or so it seemed to the home-based part of the family, struggling with new schools, new services, new terrain. However, our new flat garden was such a joy to our youngest after the precipitous slopes of Sheffield, that he spent the whole of the first summer outside. Something positive to hang on to in the face of so much that was alien. When I asked our neighbour where the nearest library was she said, "Oh, but you can't walk there, it's uphill." Uphill, after living in a Pennine town! It seemed that no one else had ever moved into or out of Northampton at that time. Our closest friends there have always lived within a mile of where they were born, except for three years in a village five miles away. They quickly returned.

Roger was entirely absorbed in starting the new business and developing co-operative decision-making procedures, and I think he must have found it hard to take on board our struggles to find out how the buses worked and where to park the car when we went into the town. Many people move at times of change in their personal lives, starting a family, starting school, beginning secondary school, apart from the prime reason for the move. None of the old supports were in place, or so it seemed to me with four young children, and I had little energy to look for new ones if they did not fall into my lap. I knew it was vital for us all that Roger took this work opportunity and that we had to do what we could to make this possible, and that there would come a time when he would do the same for me. I did not enjoy those early years in Northampton and when I look at photos of myself at that time I look dreary, and I think I was. However, marriages only survive if we recognise that when our partner has to take a distinctive step we are prepared to support them in it, whatever the cost. Even in today's climate of equal opportunities it is not always possible for both partners to make significant changes at the same time. This is what Joan Chittister calls the "spirituality of the long haul" (Chittister 1992 p.178), the foundations of which need to have been laid earlier and which then keeps us going when days are dull and others are living more glamorous lives.

℈ *Roger writes . . .*

Soon after we came to Northampton in 1968 we became part of a house group attached to the local Church of England parish church, four married couples and one single man. While most such groups are transient, perhaps meeting during Lent and then disbanding, this particular group decided to stay together and continued for fifteen years. It was very much an Anglican group because two of the members were ordained priests and two more were Readers. Because the continuity of the group enabled us to know each other well and trust each other in confidence, we found ourselves discussing in depth such subjects as spirituality, marriage, faith or lack of faith, and through this interchange the lives of all of us were significantly influenced. We called it a "cell group" and later a "house communion group" because the core of our fortnightly meetings was the eucharist celebrated in each other's houses.*

The members of the group lived in different parts of a widespread parish and some were more than a kilometre from others so that informal "over the fence" neighbourly contact was not possible, daily worship together was impracticable and events had to be planned in advance. Some of us began to feel that we could be a more effective part of the Church if we lived next door to each other and I wrote a paper in June 1974 with the title *Community Living in Weston Favell – an aunt sally* (see Appendix A, p.99), making the case for "some form of community" on biblical grounds and also economic and ecological considerations. At that time, there was widespread labour unrest and raging inflation † and some were predicting a siege economy and political meltdown, including the influential historian and civil servant Arnold Toynbee in an *Observer* article of 14 April 1974.

We discussed whether or not this was the "end-time" and perhaps Christ would return sooner rather than later, similar to the thinking of the early church in Jerusalem (Mark 13:30). Perhaps community living was a Christian response to a potentially cataclysmic situation? We discussed, but there was insufficient energy to move towards a residential community and, in the event, life in the UK did not become destabilised, people learned to live with massive inflation and Toynbee's prediction of a siege economy did not come to pass. Nor did the second coming! What did happen was that the country became more materialistic, perhaps as a reaction to the flower power of the

---

* We wrote a eucharist liturgy for small groups, *A Simple Communion – arranged for house meetings,* which was subsequently published by Daily Bread Co-operative Ltd and sold ten thousand copies in the 1980s.
† The mortgage rate reached 15% in November 1979 and again in October 1981.

swinging sixties. The established churches made few radical changes and continued to lose members. Susan and I continued as a "normal" married household and at that time we were deeply immersed in the time-consuming and sometimes traumatic occupation of bringing up teenage children. We had little spare energy. Our marriage survived this testing time and in due course the children grew into adults and moved away, to college, to work and to independent living. So plans for community living, which had lain dormant during these teenage years, were revived in 1982 by one of the members of the cell group who was in contact with the Iona Community. Iona was supporting residential communities in Scotland, called Columban Houses and these seemed similar to our tentative ideas. By this time the house group was beginning to disperse. The two ordained ministers were both moving to new pastures and four of us, two married couples, felt ready to commit ourselves to community living as a longterm project when suitable houses could be found. Michael and Anne suggested a minimum commitment of ten years, Susan and I wrote, "We see it as a twenty-year project, unfolding gradually and based on shared worship, shared possessions and shared time . . . Our inspiration comes from the Gospels and Acts 4, also from our house communion group experience and from communities such as Little Gidding. We believe that sharing and serving each other will in themselves help us to practise Jesus' law of love."

We looked at a number of houses for sale and in April 1984 found one, 144 Ardington Road, which seemed "right". But we needed three in a row, so Michael knocked on the door of 146 and the young man who answered it said, "Strange you should ask. My mother died recently and I'm selling this house. It's in tonight's paper. Come in and have a look round." Meanwhile, Roger rang the bell at 142 and the grey-haired woman who answered it said, "Strange you should ask. We're getting older and my sister and I have decided to share her house so I'm selling this one but I have not yet put it in the hands of an estate agent. Come in and have a look round." So in the space of a few weeks we completed the purchase of all three houses, 142/144/146.
If we needed a "sign", this was it (Acts 2:43).

Michael and Anne, quick to act when an idea seemed "in right ordering", sold their detached house in Weston Favell parish and moved into Ardington Road, surrounded by builders modifying the three houses to the design of our architect cell colleague, to include a community meeting room and a separate flat. On 30 June 1984, ten years after the writing of the first discussion paper, we moved into the renovated 146 and The Neighbours Community was born. We knocked down the fences to make one large shared garden and some of the neighbours (small n) said, "Why do you have to be different? Why can't you live like everyone else round here?"

The Neighbours Community is not a commune because we each have our own house or flat, nor is it a monastic house because we have not taken vows and are not necessarily celibate, frugal nor obedient. It is a community of households which is a compromise between independent living on the one hand and totally shared living on the other. It attracts people who feel called to live a more sharing lifestyle but would be unlikely to join a commune or a vowed monastic order. The household concept also makes it possible to form a community which includes single people, married couples such as ourselves, and children.

In current circumstances, both economic and religious, it is unlikely that monasteries will receive more than a handful of committed single men or single women but the community of households concept might appeal to a much larger number with a common faith and a common concern to move away from the individualism and increasingly materialistic culture which is thrust

The Neighbours Community

upon us by the media. The makers of lawn mowers are unlikely to support the kind of project in which five gardens are put together and only need one mower.

We searched for a lifestyle which is different from the congregational pattern of church on Sunday and detached living on Monday to Saturday but also one which was way short of monasticism.

Community Worship

We know of one or two Church of England parishes where the vicar is joined by some parishioners for regular daily morning prayer and we know of some Quaker midweek meetings for worship, but few members of such congregations are able to commit themselves to a daily discipline in church, making the journey in rain or snow and accepting it as a priority over household routines. When we formed The Neighbours Community in 1984 the assumption was that the members would keep their own daily prayer discipline and attend a congregational service on Sundays, the normal pattern for most lay Christians scattered over a parish or a town and constrained by work routines, midweek trains to catch, children to school. However, we soon realised that by deciding to live alongside each other in an ordinary suburban road we had the opportunity to develop a different pattern. Looking back, it is surprising that we were so slow to realise this opportunity. It was indeed a gift, a charism. By adopting the upside down idea of knocking the three original houses into one, with three interconnected households, we had formed ourselves, almost unconsciously, into a pattern similar to that of the early church in Jerusalem where the believers prayed together "each day" rather than once a week and they "broke bread at home". It seems these early Christians were adopting a different and more sharing lifestyle than that of the Temple congregation to which they continued to adhere.

So in 1986 the Community initiated morning prayers together and for twenty years we have regarded this as a core activity of our marriage. Of course, it is different from the monastic communities with which we were in touch, the Brothers at Taizé or the Benedictines at Turvey Abbey, where corporate worship is not only daily but several times each day, but if any of us had felt called to the monastic life we would not have pursued secular careers, got married or had children.

At first we used the liturgy of the Little Gidding Community (*Little Gidding Prayer Book* 1986) and later, over the years, we have written a number of morning liturgies for ourselves but we have found that no one pattern seems appropriate and each community member, leading prayers on a weekly rota, is now free to choose the form. Sometimes we read a psalm or the passage set in the Church of England lectionary, sometimes we read from other authors such as Henri Nouwen, Antony de Mello, Jean Vanier, Gerard Hughes. We may sing Taizé chants or Iona hymns and sometimes there is music with no words. Apart from the Lord's Prayer there is no fixed pattern but in all these liturgies, silence is an integral part. There is usually a space for intercessions which brings the needs of others to the attention of all of us and helps us to stand aside from the ever-present temptation to be absorbed only with our own sorrows or joys.

Throughout these changes in the form of daily prayer both Quakerism and Taizé have been frequently invoked. Taizé prayer, grounded in the prophetic interdenominational stance of the Brothers, has sometimes been a useful "parking place" for people who have decided to leave their congregation and need space, not necessarily in a church building, to find a new spiritual home. Many thousands of young people from all over the world now visit Taizé every summer and the gradual emergence of their prayer and lifestyle in the second half of the 20th century is one of the most wonderful movements in the Christian church. We hope it will continue to touch the hearts of many more people in the 21st century in the same way as it has touched us during the span of our marriage.

❡ *Susan writes . . .*

When one partner becomes a Quaker there are a number of challenges to be faced when it comes to worshipping together. Specific times of one-to-one shared worship have never been part of our marriage because our temperaments are so different. The style which speaks to one may set the other's teeth on edge, and yet, at the heart of our marriage, is our shared commitment to our journey together in faith. Silent worship is insufficient for Roger and a lot of words is too much for me! So, being part of a community where worship together is on a daily basis using a variety of liturgies, has been a special gift for us.

❡ *Roger writes . . .*

Eucharist*

At The Neighbours Community we have "shared our food gladly" (Acts 2:46), meeting frequently for meals together, sometimes buying food in bulk as an attempt at frugality and lending and borrowing food more often than is practicable in a conventional housing situation. Of course, good neighbours in any street lend and borrow, but a residential community is intentionally something more than chance neighbourliness as each other's store cupboards are open and accessible whether the neighbour is present or not.

This day to day sharing of food led the Community towards the sacramental sharing of bread and wine but this has been a significant theological difference between Susan and me. We both believe that all life is sacramental but whereas outward and visible signs with inward and spiritual meaning, such as the eucharist, continue to be a valued part of my spiritual journey, Susan accepts the Quaker view that such sacramental occasions are not necessary. For solidarity at Community meals, Quakers including Susan have taken part in numerous eucharistic occasions and have sometimes been the prime movers. Sometimes such occasions evolve spontaneously and sometimes they are planned in advance to enable us to invite visitors, particularly around Lent and Easter.

The eucharist is not so much a yes or no situation but more of a spectrum with Roman Catholics at one end, for whom the Mass is dominant and central, to Quakers at the other end. In between are Anglicans, Methodists and others who may have a different theological approach to eucharist but ensure that we do not evade the social implications of the Gospel by hiding behind the liturgy. Few Christians will deny that all life is sacramental but many will follow different paths. For a long time Quaker dress code was an outward and visible sign with an inward and spiritual meaning and for Catholics,

*The designation of Christian eucharistic occasions involving the sacramental sharing of bread and wine varies widely between denominations. Words include eucharist, Holy Communion, agapé, Lord's Supper, Mass, breaking bread. Eucharistic worship is further discussed in Chapter 5, "A Quaker Married to a Non-Quaker", and Appendix C is a short agapé liturgy sometimes used at supper by The Neighbours Community.

genuflection and the sign of the Cross continue to have sacramental significance. We note that Jesus "blessed and broke" the loaves at the feeding of the five thousand and "all ate and were filled" (Mark 6:41–2 NRSV). This first of all Christian eucharistic occasions was inclusive and all who chose to share their bread were encouraged by Jesus to do so. It was only later that the eucharist became exclusive.

At The Neighbours Community we have been grateful to ministers of a number of different denominations who have been willing to join us and preside over the distribution of bread and wine. Perhaps their willingness is an indication of grassroots yearning for unity at a time when intercommunion remains such a stumbling block at formal institutional levels. Maybe we are on our way back to more inclusive celebrations which will bear some similarity to the early church? We are grateful but it has to be said that neither Susan nor myself, Quaker or not, is any longer persuaded that an ordained minister *must* preside for a eucharistic occasion to be authentic. In our situation the bread has usually been baked by Susan in our kitchen and the Fairtrade wine comes from the local Co-op store. It seems appropriate to us that the service should sometimes be led by the baker or the shopper.

Denominations

When we started discussing the possibility of transforming the cell group, which lived in houses scattered over a parish, into a residential community, it was still a totally Anglican project and the founding four of us who eventually bought the houses in Ardington Road, were all attached to the Church of England, some more tightly attached than others. However, an early decision, taken with little discussion and no dissension, was that the Community was to be ecumenical and interdenominational. Later we wrote a formal statement of purpose:

> Our purpose is to develop a community life which enables us to explore and share our faith and care for others according to the gospel. Our wider aims are to encourage Christian unity and community and to seek understanding with those of other faiths.

When we added a fourth house in 1986 we were joined by a young Methodist couple and the fifth house was bought by a Roman Catholic who stayed for seven years and married a Quaker. When the Methodists left for him to train for the ministry in Birmingham, their house was bought by an Anglican couple who also stayed for seven years before moving to a parish for her to complete her training for the Anglican priesthood. Meanwhile, Susan had joined Friends and another couple, who came to the Community as a Roman Catholic married to a Baptist, both became Attenders at Northampton Quaker Meeting together with their children. These and similar changes over a period of twenty years have underpinned the ecumenical focus of our married life together and that of the Community, which has included five different denominations at one time or another. We may have changed our view of the primacy and indispensability of the clergy as intermediaries between mankind and God but we have also often given thanks that close friends have responded to their call to professional ministry and we have done what we can to support them during the demanding time of training and change of lifestyle.

Varying denominational views have enhanced rather than diminished our life together and though we have had arguments, like most married couples, our differences have seldom been about denominational matters. The Neighbours Community, which has been a central part of our life together, founded by churchgoers and defined by its worship, has always been Christocentric and it is Jesus' teaching in the Gospels that has brought us to unity and held us together.

From a Friends' perspective the weakness of our denominational diversity is that, unlike the Quaker communities at Bamford in the UK or Pendle Hill in the USA there has been no agenda to develop a lifestyle specifically incorporating the testimonies of peace, simplicity, truth, equality and community.* We have silent worship, sometimes Quaker grace, sometimes Bible sharing groups in Lent, but these are mixed in with liturgies from other sources such as Taizé, Iona and the Book of Common Prayer.

During the 1980s, Susan tried out several congregations within walking distance of our new house and, for a time, found a tentative

---

* To the historic testimonies, some Quaker authors now add "community". See for example Griswold 2005.

home with an independent evangelical church which met at our local primary school. However, before long, she realised that her true spiritual home was Quakerism and she became an Attender and then a Member of Northampton Quaker Meeting in 1989. She is an active Quaker, holding various offices locally, co-ordinating the writing of a book, *This is Who I Am: Listening with Older Friends,* published by Quaker Books in 2003, and being a tutor at Woodbrooke where we were both invited to be Friends in Residence in 1992.

These denominational changes reflect changes in our beliefs and unbeliefs. In 1957 we would both probably have recited the Nicene creed without perjuring ourselves but, as the years rolled by and we gained both knowledge from reading and experience from relationships, neither of us would now adhere to some of the less biblically-based clauses. There are positive changes too. Susan has read widely on the search for the historical Jesus, particularly the American theologians who have shed so much new light during the latter half of the 20th century. She would choose her words carefully regarding the divinity of Jesus but both of us would acknowledge the centrality of the Gospels as unique records. Across the spectrum of Christian belief both of us would say that we believe more and more about less and less, hopefully throwing off some of the dubious accretions which churches and their priests have added over the last two millennia. This is not to say that either of us have become fundamentalist Christians. Far from it, because the Gospels are too full of parables and cultural innuendoes for there to be any reliable literal meaning for some of the more obscure passages. To take a simple example, in Matthew 26:61 Jesus says he can destroy the Temple and rebuild it in three days. As it had taken the Jews forty years to build it, this would be an impossible constructional task but Jesus was speaking of his own body as a "Temple of God".

We attend prayers together nearly every day and often go to church services together so, although our priorities differ, this has not caused any sense of separation in our marriage. At best it has sharpened the continuous debate about finding God and the worst that can be said is that it complicates our routines, with Susan heading towards the meeting house on Sundays and me towards the soup kitchen as a voluntary helper.

Susan, influenced by her reading of the Quaker texts, and me too from observing the fragility as well as the gifts of clergy whom we have known well, are hesitant about relying on ordained ministers and we both testify to the dangers of tying ourselves to religious doctrines proclaimed as true mainly by ecclesiastical authorities. Such doctrines need to be tested against the Gospels time after time and against the lives of God-fearing people age after age, laity as much as clergy. Friends at London Yearly Meeting in 1986 declared, "To be without ordained clergy is not to be without either leadership or ministry. The gifts of the Spirit to us include both." (*QFP* 12.02) So it may be more accurate to say that Quakers have not so much done away with ministers but they have done away with the laity (*QFP* 11.01). They ask, "What canst *thou* say?" (*QFP* 19.07), meaning that personal experience is often a truer guide than dogma.

We both found the lifestyle of the suburban Church of England congregations of which we were part in Sheffield and then in Northampton, increasingly constraining and we looked for a theology and a lifestyle which would take more account of Jesus' teaching about justice. Susan, for example, was incensed that the Anglican church relegated women to a secondary ministry and refused to ordain them as priests. They were marginalised and their gifts often ignored by the male-dominated clergy. She joined the Movement for the Ordination of Women (MOW) and though she did not chain herself to church railings she became an activist along with others and was overjoyed at the first ordination of women in 1994. She did not sense a call to ordination herself but moved towards the Quakers who had no ordained ministers. *Quaker Faith and Practice* 19.31 quotes George Fox:

What! are all true Christians priests? Yes. What! are women priests? Yes, women priests.

It has been Quaker practice for many years to make as few distinctions as possible between men and women when appointing people to positions of responsibility and this is taken for granted in all the numerous groups which are part of the Religious Society of Friends. In Quaker-speak, the absence of gender distinctions in the work of the Society is "in right ordering".

A further denominational influence came to us from visits to Turvey Abbey, a Benedictine monastery near Bedford, and later to another one on Shaw Island off the west coast of the USA. The rhythm of alternate prayer and manual work throughout the day seemed appropriate for a Christian community. Benedict taught that the prayer is the work and the manual work is also prayer. This led us to incorporate daily prayers into the Neighbours Community lifestyle. Visits to a remote Greek island brought us in touch with the Greek Orthodox church and we played a small part in the restoration of an isolated monastery there, visiting it nearly every year since 1992. Our ecumenical experiences lead us to the view that the unity for which Jesus prayed, "that they may be one" (John 17:21) is just as likely to come from the bottom upwards as from the top downwards. Formal statements of unity from ecclesiastical authorities are important but rather than giving a lead to people in the pews, henceforward they may be formulating what is already happening at the grassroots.

In conclusion, our spiritual journeys have been a dominant part of our marriage and encompass a wide ecumenical and interdenominational sweep. The most significant influences for both of us have been the Sheffield Industrial Mission, the Taizé Community, our membership of The Neighbours Community for over twenty years, and for Susan her membership of the Religious Society of Friends (Quakers), all of which bear witness to the Gospel

of love and compassion for our fellow men and women, particularly the marginalised and dispossessed. Our face to face wisdom-figures have been Ted Wickham (Anglican), George MacLeod (Church of Scotland), Frère Jan (Taizé Communauté), for speaking truth to power; Ken Thomason (Baptist), Janey O'Shea (Quaker), Charlie Moule (Anglican), for personal discipleship and understanding of life's purpose.

3 Marriage – Susan

Some Historical Reflections

To what purpose did the creator of mankind first divide our human race into two sexes, male and female, and then implant in each a strong desire for association and union with each other? Is it not plain that he wished the two to be united and live together and by their joint efforts to devise a way of life in common?

Musonius Rufus, 35–100 CE (Coleman 2004)

In New Testament times, Paul had this to say:

> For this reason a man will leave his father and mother and be joined to his wife, and the two will become one flesh (Ephesians 5:31)

> So then he who marries his fiancée does well; and he who refrains from marriage will do better. (1 Corinthians 7:38)

There has always been a tension between marriage and celibacy in the religious life. Paul struggled with this issue, seemingly endorsing marriage when writing to the Ephesians and discouraging it when writing to the Corinthians. There is a charmingly human quotation in 1 Corinthians 9:5 where he grumbles that Peter and Jesus' brothers take their wives with them on their travels so why shouldn't he take a Christian brother with him? Paul was human after all! I find it a great comfort to learn that Augustine was struggling with some of the same dilemmas we struggle with at present, one of which has only recently been resolved by the Civil Partnership Act which enables same-sex partners to have some legal standing.

> If a man and a woman live together without being legitimately joined, not to have children, but because they could not observe continence, and if they have agreed between themselves to have relations with no one else, can this be called a marriage?

> Augustine, 4th century CE (Coleman 2004)

Marriage was seen as part of the Natural Law, a law not peculiar to the human race but shared by all creatures, the union of male and female and the production of offspring. Indeed the consent to be married carried with it an agreement to consummate the marriage sexually and this consummation was the sacrament, the ministers of the sacrament of marriage being the couple themselves. The possibility of a specifically Christian way of getting married only appears from the 5th century onwards and the rule that Christian marriage should be accomplished by exchanging promises at the church porch, supervised and witnessed by a priest, with a nuptial Mass to follow if the couple chose, was not firmly established in the west until the 13th century, and even in the 15th century about half the population still married by family or private agreement rather than in church.

Come the Reformation, Luther and Calvin opposed the church's authority over matrimonial law, believing it to be rightly the concern of "the godly state". When the Church of England tried to sort out the procedures by means of the Hardwick Act of 1756, making it obligatory that all marriages take place within the Church of England, the only exceptions were the Quakers and the Jews. The Quakers as early as 1656 were asking meetings to set up ways to cover the marriage of members, to oversee and record weddings, which was vital for the legal status and property rights of children. In 1659 a minute was passed as to marriage procedures, providing for public notice of intention at General Meeting or at the end of the meeting to which the parties belonged. The marriage to be solemnised at a meeting of not less than ten Friends and registered and the Certificate of Marriage shown to a public magistrate soon afterwards, thus conforming as soon as possible to the law then in force. In 1668 George Fox took steps to strengthen the marriage procedures of Friends by bringing marriages under the direct care of monthly meetings who were to reprove persons married by a priest (Braithwaite 1923).

Thomas Corbett, a Welsh lawyer sympathetic to Friends, in 1679 concluded that if a man and a woman agreed to take each other as man and wife for life but without an ordained minister nor using the form presented by the Book of Common Prayer, it was a legal marriage as the civil law favoured mutual consent (Horle 1988).

The earliest Christian churches were dependent on the protection of married households, just as in Puritan times companionate marriage was seen to provide a "harmonious background for the spiritual life" (Hayden 2002). Nevertheless in the 3rd and 4th centuries ambitious, younger, poorer people could rise to leadership positions in the church through the ideal of chastity at the expense of rich heads of families, whose divided loyalties were seen as a hindrance to the call of the religious life. Sanctified marriage lost its central role in the church hierarchy and the ideal became the "mystique of continence" which we can still see today in the two-tier system both in the Roman Catholic and Orthodox churches and in other faith traditions, the wandering Sadhu and the Buddhist monk to name but two. In the Orthodox church one must marry before becoming a parish priest but only celibate monks can become bishops.

When early Quakers married the idea that they should travel in married partnership was discouraged although Friends of mature years, like Thomas and Anne Camm, sometimes did so. To marry was to accept some degree of limitation. The social bonds that tied the believer to marriage and through marriage to the framework of the state prejudiced the mission of spreading the "Good News".

Transformation

Thomas Moore* writes that marriage is a vessel of transformation, a place of development of the soul, deep non-rational connections allowing the process of fermentation, the blending of opposites to produce rich wine (Moore 2004 p.153). He refers to this as alchemy, the pseudo-scientific predecessor of chemistry that sought a method of transmuting base metal into gold. That is what the mystery of marriage can do, transmute base metal into gold. What a claim!

In John's Gospel, Jesus' first public sign was at a wedding, where he changed water into wine, not only saving the bridegroom from embarrassment but showing that in the marriage change will take place.

A young friend who was staying with us kept asking, "What do you do to sustain a long marriage? And is it worth it?" Perhaps these are the wrong questions. It is not so much what we are doing but what

---

* A present day psychotherapist and not to be confused with Sir Thomas More (1478–1535).

is being done within this transforming vessel because, for sure, nothing causes such a shift in your lifestyle as being open to the alchemy of marriage. Of course we may choose to lead parallel lives, never quite committing ourselves to entering with heart and soul into the "vessel", but it feels as if another alchemy is at work if we make this choice, a hardening and rigidity creating brittleness and a "box without a key" rather than a vessel from which gold can be poured.

Our wedding

Getting Married in 1957 – Staying Married until 2006

I wish I could recall the accepted customs around marriage in 1957 but I have only rather hazy memories of that time. Our expectation was that we were marrying for life and that society and the Church supported this ideal.

We knew few people who were divorced. I recollect exotically risqué images of silk-stockinged legs crossed at the knee, sitting on bar stools with a long cigarette holder between bright red lips and a cocktail at hand. Or sinister men in raincoats, trilby hats pulled over their faces, loitering in doorways, looking for evidence of the guilty party "at it". Yes, it was that unreal and we had no direct experience of such happenings.

If I had thought about marriage in an analytical way I suppose I would have identified older people who appeared unhappy in their marriage, "unequally yoked", but who stumbled on, often living apparently separate lives. The thought that they might divorce would have shocked me. People were not always blissfully happy, that was adult life and society expected them to get on with it as best they could.

Single people were a satellite group. I was taught by powerful but slightly warped women, many of whom would have married but for the ravages of the First World War. My housemistress was a lively rather waspish woman who flirted with the girls' visiting fathers, it was rumoured that the headmistress and the drama teacher were a couple, our deputy housemistress was a spinster plain to see. We took all these permutations for granted.

During the Second World War many women had managed on their own. A friend says of her widowed mother, "She modelled for me that women could manage." When the euphoria of peace had evaporated and women had returned to domesticity, many began to question their assigned role but in order to get out of a life-denying marriage they had to run the gauntlet of the existing divorce laws, which required extraordinary evidence to prove that the marriage had broken down, the most acceptable cause being adultery. Divorce was seen to put you outside society and your image became impossibly tarnished. It was also difficult at that time for women to support themselves and their children.

Birth control was a very inexact science, all those rubber caps in pink boxes and creams and trying to get the wretched thing in place. No wonder there were so many unintentional pregnancies and once you were pregnant you had to go through with it. Abortion happened dangerously in back streets.

In Roman times only two out of every ten live births survived to adulthood but in the 1950s we were balanced on the cusp of change. Childbirth was safer and more children survived. There was no realisation that the world was overpopulated but also it was not seen as imperative to replace the population. We had children because we wanted to have them and we did not weigh up the cost of rearing them. In later years we felt we had to apologise for our large families.

Adaptation or Sacrifice?

Thomas Moore tells us "Together you become mingled souls". "Sacrifice" seems too dramatic a description, and smells of the Temple and bleating lambs and fatted calves – not a 21st century word. However, it seems inevitable that some of our hopes, habits and pleasures will be given up in the good cause of our "mingled souls". In the case of early Friends real sacrifices were made, but did we make sacrifices, I wonder? Adaptations, yes, and probably some of the things we had to lay down were painful but surely not to the point of death. Or maybe they were little deaths, the ways we did not go because we chose to go the same way.

"In marriage there is only room for one partner to fly," a friend responded when asked how things were for him. "My wife is flying whereas I feel as if I have my elbows clamped to my sides." It is surely impossible to have a lifelong relationship without a large measure of adaptation. Our son and his partner were debating where they might live in Seattle and listening in on the discussion I realised how much adjustment there has to be to accommodate two differing life courses, and to attempt a decision where both can live and grow and have their being and fulfil at least some of their dreams. This entails sacrificing other dreams but I am struck again by the enormity of the word sacrifice. It seems too large a concept for the choices that have to be made. Do we go for a house or a flat? Do we stay in the central and therefore expensive area of the city or move further out to a cheaper area where we can afford more space but are dependent on a car? Lifestyle choices: but hardly the choices Elizabeth Gurney had to make when deciding whether she should marry Joseph Fry. In Jean Hatton's description, "In his absence she missed him . . . yet too much of him still annoyed her and she often felt her time better spent with her poor people or her school" (Hatton 2005).

Roger gave up his commitment to cricket as I was temperamentally unsuited to being a cricket wife. Hardly martyrdom. What were my major adaptations? I suppose learning to look after someone who I felt had a very clear vision of where he wanted his life to go and I wanted to support him in this. I returned to the Anglican church for although Roger had never seen his church membership in terms of the parish, his affiliation was definitely within the Anglican orbit, primarily through the Sheffield Industrial Mission which, despite its claims to be interdenominational, was deeply rooted in the Church of England. I had left my public school Anglicanism for the Presbyterian church which was the orbit of the Iona Community. I had been involved with Iona since college days, leading me to the Industrial Mission and thence to Roger. To say that it was a sacrifice to return to my Anglican roots would be giving this move too great a significance. It was part of my wish that our faith journey should be united and our children raised in one religious family, and they were greatly blessed by this connection. I was espoused to no great cause on which I had to turn my back in order to be a home-maker and the idea of continuing my work as an occupational therapist never crossed my mind. I remember being shocked when our neighbour in Sheffield was so consumed by the pre-school playgroup movement that she largely left her Methodist minister husband to do most of the child care. This was my first encounter with someone unwilling to sacrifice their career aspirations in order to fulfil what was at that time seen to be the wife's role. Now it is taken for granted that the sacrifice, if that is what it is, should be mutual.

According to Jung, "True love involves sacrifice of potential" (Jung 1928). Is he saying that it is impossible for those of huge potential to fulfil this within marriage? Perhaps so, as we must all know people we feel should never have married because their drive to fulfil their potential is so strong that unless there are huge sacrifices on the part of their partner their relationship will end in disaster. Nevertheless the sacrifice can bring rewards in shared satisfaction as the vision comes to fruition. There have been periods when Roger has been developing new ideas and bringing to fruition new projects, when the family have been well aware that they have "come second to the vision", as one of our daughters put it. Christine Trevett describes how "when publicly active Quakers married they would soon find themselves separated . . . travelling in married partnership was discouraged in the 17th century" (Trevett 1991).

Adapting is inevitable, someone has to sleep on the wrong side of the bed. Two lifestyles attempting to coalesce involve change and modification. It is the nitty-gritty of living together that can be corrosive if we are not careful. Roger hates duvets, they make him too hot, so we soldier on with the blankets my mother bought us on our marriage, by now much darned (I keep telling our children I want one for a shroud). Are we a coffee or tea drinking family, when do we have our meals? The everyday routines can be very different in the families we come from and the creation of a new one can cause unforeseen culture clashes and an accumulation of niggles, leaving one partner feeling undervalued and overwhelmed. As we grow older we are in a continual state of adaptation to which we have hopefully become more accustomed. There will always be sticking points. I am not an intrepid Third World traveller so Roger must do that bit on his own. He does not put any priority on going to concerts but we must never make assumptions, because we change and suddenly feel hurt because it is assumed we don't want to go to the concert on Friday. Oh dear, it is all such hard work and if we are not constantly checking, we are in danger of slipping apart and all the previous sacrifices and adaptations will have been in vain.

In Jesus we see God's commitment to the world. "All things have been handed over to me" (Matthew 11:27) and our symbolic commitment to another in some mysterious way encapsulates all that this can mean in a lived and committed life to that most earthed of relationships. "Marriage, like household slavery, was a calling devoid of glamour," writes Peter Brown about the 2nd century CE (Brown 1988). We need not go as far as that but procreation, the handing on of property, the bodily, financial and spiritual care of one person for another in the most intimate of ways, reflects the particular emphasis of the Judaeo-Christian tradition. On consideration, it feels like a huge step, a step away from autonomy by handing over your life to the safekeeping of another and receiving theirs in the presence of God and the meeting, but it can be a step into new life.

Community Living and Marriage

For Martin Buber, "The community of marriage is part of the greater community, joining with its own problems the general problems" (Buber 1947 p.71). Married couples can be seen to be exclusive and to exclude other members of a community. "The single people orbited the married couples," was how a member of the Catholic Worker Movement described a community she joined. But sometimes intentional communities depend on a core of married people, two for the price of one. Martin Buber sees the community of marriage as the commitment to being answerable to the other, the decisive entering into relating to others which is the absolute basis of community. Being woven together.

The Neighbours Community has not always been successful in creating a level playing field for people living alone, at one end of the field, and those in families at the other end. When the weekly meeting is over some go home and can discuss what happened with their partner or be diverted by the demands of their children and some are left to ponder on their own. Community living is not a panacea for aloneness. Perhaps one of the criteria for living in community, as in marriage, is the ability to be alone. We received a phone call on New Year's Day, "I am sick of living alone. Can I come and visit your community?" Not a good start for exploring community living!

In the community of the Quaker meeting there are usually many "single ones", especially Quakers married to non-Quakers, so there is less exclusivity. But the final reference point is nearly always the other, the partner, and therefore the commitment to the community of the meeting is dependent on the cooperation of the non-Quaker. A member of our meeting must be home for lunch at one o'clock, his Methodist wife has a less demanding timetable.

In these days when there is a lessening of a feeling of wider community, marriages often bear the burden of being the only community for many people and the way this impinges on the unwillingly single, living alone, surrounded by strangers, is one that needs addressing. I remember coming upon a member of our meeting in Waterstones one Sunday. I asked her what she was looking for. "Filling in time before going home to lunch on my own," said this successful, attractive woman with many friends. For some years, The Neighbours tried to address Sunday isolation by having open house at teatime and it was our least favourite commitment. In 2004 we decided to lay it down, feeling it had outrun its usefulness. It had become bogged down with a group of people who were so dysfunctional that each one wanted undivided attention and certainly was not interested in anyone else who might come, so they did not.

Roger and I once took part in a retreat for Teams of Our Lady, a largely Roman Catholic organisation for the support of marriage. Every time I chose to sit apart from Roger someone would ask where he was and where would he sit? I replied that I could sit with him anytime and would like a change! I realise that that is my luxury.

Marriage – The Legal Contract

George Fox said, "We marry none, it is the Lord's work, we are but witnesses" (*Quaker Faith and Practice* 16.01). Quakers have always tried to regulate the marriage procedure within the current legislation, while staying true to their principles. It must say something about the value society puts on marriage that it seeks to bring it within the legal framework and root it in the community. In the USA it is legally permitted to marry anywhere provided a legally-approved minister is present, except that in the state of Alaska, where there are small isolated communities, it is only necessary to have two other people present as witnesses in order that the marriage should be recognised in law. It seems that even in such a remote place it is accepted that a legal marriage is a community commitment, assisting the stability of the community, and that these witnesses make it a formal agreement between the couple and the body politic.

Nevertheless as with other key words associated with marriage the word "contract" has negative associations of restriction, downsizing and shortening. All words of diminishment rather than enhancement. It seems that those of us long-married must find the energy within the perceived contractions, as in childbirth. That is the challenge and something that seems less and less valued and understood. "Don't fence me in", even if the fence enables me to be secure and rooted. Looking at the cows and llamas in the field below the guesthouse of a Benedictine monastery, fenced in so that each has the pasture which will provide the nourishment to make them strong and healthy so they can produce healthy offspring, I can see the value of imposed limits. I imagine cows and llamas look at the woods on the other side of the fence and long to wander off and indeed some of them succeed, but they don't last long for, like the uncontrolled deer, they are in danger of being hit by a car or shot.

Marriage is a legal contract but as members of a religious society we believe that the drawing together of people into this contract is "the work of the Lord". Despite alarmingly high divorce statistics people still feel they want this legal contract with one another and in many cases that it should take place within a religious framework, which they often do not subscribe to and do not have any contact with on a day to day basis. An attractive setting clearly influences their choice. The brutally modern church, set in a local shopping complex, has few non-congregants married there, whereas the neighbouring ancient parish church has a waiting list. Despite our cynicism at the reasons for choosing a church wedding there must be an underlying feeling that taking this step, to make what in all probability is already a marriage in all but name (and often with children, as in Posy Simmonds' cartoon, p.50) into a legally-binding relationship with some expectation of a lifelong commitment, needs all the help it can get, including God and a great cloud of witnesses. Whether the religious institutions are rising to the challenge is a moot point. A friend, who is a vicar in the diocese of St Albans, tells some pertinent stories about couples coming to his church for marriage preparation. One young woman asked if you could get married if you had not lived together first. Another couple were asked if they wanted their second child baptised before or after their wedding ceremony. "Before," they said. "The first one was a bastard so she better be one as well," and they all trooped up to the chancel steps from the font! The Roman Catholic diocese of Northampton will not allow couples to be married unless they have attended a marriage preparation course. How about that, Friends?

Cartoon by Posy Simmonds

© Posy Simmonds Reproduced with permission

In some subtle way the step from cohabitation to legal commitment seems to change the way the relationship functions. A friend of one of our daughters, amazed at the length of our marriage, clearly saw that her own long term relationship, with children, was the seedbed for a legal contract, which she now felt ready to undertake. Her view contrasted with the conventional concept of a legal marriage first, with the hope that a long term relationship will develop and certainly that children will be born.

That acute observer of the human condition, Anne Tyler, writes:

> I knew couples who had been married almost forever . . . forty, fifty, sixty years. Seventy two in one case. They'd been tending each other's illnesses, filling each other's faulty memories, dealing with money troubles or the daughter's suicide or the grandson's drug addiction. And I was beginning to suspect it made no difference whether they had married the right person. Finally you are just with who you're with. You signed on with her, put in half a century with her, grown to know her as well as you know yourself or even better, and she has become the right person. Or the only person might be more to the point . . . (Tyler 1999 p.219)

The Gift of Grace

"Grace evokes our acts, supports them, fulfils them, something that we cannot handle on our own but only with the help and support of God" (De Waal 1984 p.62). The idea of grace seems to be relevant only in a religious setting but perhaps the word serendipity is a non-religious equivalent. De Waal stresses that this gift of God, this unmerited gift, unsought, is not something passive. "By the grace of God" is a call to action not a fait accompli.

"Surprised by grace" is how I felt when Roger asked me to marry him! How come that this amazing man wanted to marry me and how can I be for him what he requires? In *Quaker Faith & Practice* 22.34, Elise Boulding confesses that she had "somehow to reconstruct herself to be a person worthy of such a venture" and this was my position entirely, which I now see can lead to all sorts of difficult and in some cases destructive paths. I can spend all my energy being for the other what I feel he requires of me and eventually getting to the stage where my life is subsumed by his needs so that I no longer have any independent existence. The energy all goes one way and there is no synergy. Observing friends who thought, at marriage, that they would be the gift that would alleviate their partner's addiction, mental illness, sexual ambiguity, etc, I realise this needs a different sort of grace.

We eventually have to be aware that our partner is also "graced" by us and our gifts and we are denying "that of God in us" if we do not develop our own gifts. The grace is in the uniting and then it is up to us. Luther married because he believed that in marriage God's grace permeated the world. This is where marriage within a faith setting differs most from secular marriage. By God's grace we are a gift for one another, recognising that this person is the person with whom I can create a relationship that will deepen, grow and last a lifetime. This is the dimension within the relationship which earths us in the created world, connects us with the community and is open to the transcendent.

Life Partnership – A Partnership for Giving Life

There are many ways of drawing upon the invisible resources of the universe and of releasing energy to live by.
(Jones 1921 p.xxiv)

A partnership for the duration of one's life has little merit, except for endurance, unless it is a life-giving partnership. Admiration for our nearly fifty years of married life together is hollow unless what this partnership has produced gives life to each of us, to our children and grandchildren and to those with whom we have had the privilege of living in community. It is very easy to sink into a low level of existence, side by side, indeed sharing most of how one lives but really having very little mutual energy and giving little mutual support, bickering bad temperedly about the minutiae of life and continually irritable with one another. Partnership feels so positive. "My life will be better if I live with you". Better than what? Bob Geldof talks of the cosiness of marriage, of coming home to a meal at the end of an awful day. Of course that is life enhancing, the sheer comfort factor of living together for a long time, the routines you build, who does what, no questions asked, just do it. However these tried and tested mechanics of living together can also be an elephant trap, denying one another the opportunity for growth, creating such interdependence that when one partner dies the other can hardly function.

Conversely we can get into the situation which suits one partner and denies the other. In my work as an occupational therapist I would meet couples where on retirement the husband would gradually annexe the wife's roles and eventually she would become an invalid to whom he ministered – his work. Then he died, which was where we came in, the invalid widow with no independence. Could we rehabilitate her? Miracles happened, I have seen both men and women rise from the dependent role created for them and take up a new life. Beware! We need to be constantly checking what we are doing to one another, are we truly partners, mutual dependents, or is one partner caged in to a more dependent role?

Mutual dependency seems inevitable in a long relationship. Inevitably we come to rely on one another. When someone phoned and asked for me, to discuss an annuity, I have to confess that I went and fetched Roger. I am not proud of that fact. I am dependent on Roger in financial matters. One of our daughters keeps urging me to teach him to cook. "If you die first, Mum, he will die of starvation!" Actually he is an adequate cook. Our children's marriages seem much less gender specific and our sons-in-law are good cooks and iron their own shirts. They wear them, of course, so how ridiculous to think otherwise but us fifty years marrieds didn't think like this. Women did the ironing, men managed the money and the car and there were grey areas like gardening and decorating. How antiquated it all seems. But I need consciously to develop areas of independence and autonomy. Some day I may need to manage my own finances and be responsible for the car. I watch with awe as a recently separated member of our Community takes responsibility for all areas of her life and this makes me aware that I shelter under the umbrella of the roles we have almost unconsciously assigned to one another over fifty years.

One of my dangers is of assigning the role of "moral superiority" to Roger and I become the "naughty girl". Good friends of ours, both pastors and theologians, exemplify this for me. He is a lover of music and collects records about which he is uncharacteristically ill-disciplined. When he is feeling guilty about buying them he smuggles them into the house without his wife knowing and then suggests lending them to me to make him feel better! The trouble is we both like the same music and I usually have them already. It is all fairly childish and adds a bit of spice to life but it can become corrosive, not least for the one assigned to be the keeper of morality who may feel the need for a massive breakout which could endanger the stability of the whole enterprise.

Marriage as Sacrament

Thomas Moore writes, "The mystery of marriage is eternal" (Moore 2004 p.163). I find it difficult to see how the idea of a long marriage can be supported except in the context of "sacrament". In seeing marriage within the religious/spiritual framework one can have a working hypothesis that something of an inward, transforming nature will take place, through grace, the gift which godwardness bestows on the process. The lifelong commitment to discover this gift is what makes the idea of a long marriage worthwhile.

Kierkegaard, Byron and Jung at one time or another have described a long relationship as "hell", or "sacrifice", or "a prison". Nevertheless, Jung also regarded "a full, stable and lasting relationship to be not only satisfying, enriching and a source of happiness" but called it "a true and undeniable experience of divinity" (Wallis 1988 p.128).

We certainly shared the belief that marriage is a religious act (and I suppose that could include the possibility that it could be "hell"!) and we agree with *Quaker Faith and Practice* that "the love which unites man and woman is part of the great love of God" (*QFP* 22.37). An outward and visible sign of an inward mystery rather than a prison and we were prepared to accept that sacrifice was part of the process.

Elizabeth Schüssler Fiorenza contends that for Paul, both marriage and freedom from marriage are charisms from God (Fiorenza 1983).

Stability, Fidelity, Limitation

A friend's husband died and she said she would not marry again, "it required too much effort!" She was joking of course and eventually did remarry, but there is truth in her joke, it does require effort and if we do not put effort in the relationship dies or becomes the duty Kierkegaard dreaded (Gardiner 2002 p.46). I think I thrive on limitations. I often think I chose to be a weaver because of the limitation of the basic right angle of warp over weft. Any distortion of this produces an intrinsically unstable fabric.

The Benedictines take a vow of "Stability". "True happiness cannot necessarily be found anywhere else than in this place at this time," says Dom Columban Byre (in De Waal 1984 p.57). God is not elsewhere. Just as learning to live in the present is one of life's tasks, so finding love with whom one has chosen for life is another. Rushing round searching for the perfect partner is unlikely to yield up richer fruits than accepting the imperfections in the partner you have chosen.

After we returned from a long overland journey to Israel in 1967, people would say, "That must have been wonderful," to which I would reply bad-temperedly, "Yes, but I took myself with me!" For you may travel to the ends of the earth but unless you are happy travelling with yourself you can gain nothing. Conversely you can spend most of your life with one person and gain the whole world.

Individualism and Spiritual Adultery

Jack Wallis writes: "Jung regarded a full, stable and lasting relationship in marriage (or the equivalent) to be not only satisfying, enriching and a source of happiness. He called it "a true and undeniable source of divinity, the transcending power which blots out and consumes everything individual" (Wallis 1988 p.128).

The rise of individualism is seen as a direct challenge to the ideal of a long marriage. Can we remain our own person, allow our partner to be their own person and sustain a long marriage? Despite Jung citing marriage as "a true and undeniable experience of divinity", when his wife had died he felt "an inner obligation to become what I myself am" (Storr 1973 p.10).

I have often told the story of how, at the age of thirty-six and after eleven years of marriage, I woke up one morning and thought, "I am just as good as Roger!" Pathetic isn't it? I married knowing I was marrying someone whom others, as well as myself, saw as especially gifted, in whom they had great trust, which was not how I saw myself. Competent, yes, practical, with the ability to be a good homemaker, but not with the gifts I recognised in Roger. It took me eleven years to see that both of us needed me to put some energy into discovering my own gifts other than those that contributed directly to family life, and that I would need to negotiate the freedom to do this. Something that is taken for granted these days, the raising of children in tandem with a career and the individual journeys of both partners, the logistics of which are shared.

Roger and I disagree about this. He feels that the stress of trying to combine a demanding career job together with being the main carer for four school-age children would have been detrimental both to the children and the job. I, unrepentant feminist that I am, feel that both women and men should have the right to work, if they choose. But I accept the difficulties and as grandparents we are called upon to be part of the solution, as each of our three daughters is combining demanding career work with bringing up children. Their husbands are more involved with child rearing than Roger was at that stage of family life.

There may only be room for one partner "to fly" and it takes real effort to make sure you are both sharing in the flight, otherwise there is a danger of "spiritual adultery". *Quaker Faith and Practice* 22.49 states: "Unfaithfulness is not necessarily physical. There is a kind of mental or spiritual adultery which can damage all the people concerned . . . if it creates a sense of exclusion and disorientation, and destroys the confidence, respect and affection promised in marriage."

The journey of the soul can lead one into intense friendships. Perhaps women are more susceptible to this but it applies to men as well. The myth is that the married man is looking for the younger woman, the ideal sexual partner, enhancer of his virility, lost in the demands of marriage and child rearing. The camaraderie of the sports club is a different sort of relationship but no less exclusive in terms of engagement with where we are at and the sharing of our deepest desires. The comfortable bonhomie of the swimming pool changing room, the jacuzzi and the bar seem a specifically masculine form of bonding. Women share their souls but the soul shared through sport is no less binding. "Did we give you permission to be away?" was how Roger was greeted after four weeks away from his usual swimming slot. Let us not underestimate the bond of such shared experiences and the possibility of draining away intimacy from the marriage if this is a more congenial place to share your soul, to share the core experiences, generating energy with another, excluding the married partner from the excitement, discovery and growth.

Roger is administrator of a charitable fund making grants in Eritrea and has travelled there a number of times, sometimes with friends from home. People ask me why I do not go with him and I always reply that it is what he does on his own or with someone other than his wife. I think I enjoy hearing about it more than experiencing it. He is unlikely ever to become a Quaker, his spiritual journey needs a different landscape but he is glad I have found the right one for mine. We have to develop both the intimacy and the individualism, to allow the space and share the discoveries.

I asked a Friend if she was missing coming to meeting with her husband now that he had decided to return to his previous church. She said, "We have to develop the space between us as well as the togetherness so we can function as individuals," and pointed me to some lines from *The Prophet* by Kahlil Gibran, which was read at their wedding:

> But let there be spaces in your togetherness
> And let the winds of heaven dance between you

If our marriages are to be the engine house of our lives, where the energy for living is generated, some of the fuel will come from encounters with others but it all goes into the same furnace.

Mutual/Unconditional/Intimate

When I was growing up we would talk endlessly about who we would marry. Our suitor would get down on one knee and ask, "Will you marry me?", to which I imagined replying, "Yes, if you have twins in the family." In the event we were crouching under a bush, in a snow storm, above Rivelin dam near Sheffield. It was May 1957 and Roger had no twins in his family and it is part of the legend that he had made a list of the areas in which I could improve, which we discussed outside the Glossop Road baths. He was right, there was definitely room for change. Of course I thought he was perfect! Hardly a demonstration of unconditionality.

My favourite mutuality story is of friends who were chaplain and secretary to Geoffrey Fisher, Archbishop of Canterbury. The Archbishop came upon Michael turning the handle of Anne's sewing machine and said, "We can't have that kind of thing going on here. You'd better get married", and they did. Intimate acts followed!

What goes into building a relationship of personal intimacy rooted in trust? It is a function of time and permanence, a sharing of experiences, tastes and dreams and hopes for the future and fears from the past, says Rollo May, who considers that the anxiety generated by intimate relationships is the particular problem of our day. The sharing of ourselves with another and then continuing to live with them day by day (May 1972 p.50).

We can be in danger of boring each other silly, especially as we get older. The same stories, the same opinions, lead to the temptation to stop really listening and not invest prime time in being with one another. My parents always sat down at the end of the day, with a gin and tonic, and told each other what the day had been like for them. A valuable model for me, but difficult to stick to during our child-rearing and work-dominated years. And neither of us likes gin! One of the many good things our children do for one another is to have their nieces and nephews for the weekend so each set of parents gets time together without the children, thus building the habit of intimacy.

Preparing the Ingredients

When we were writing this, young friends said, "People will want to know how you prepared for your marriage," and "What are the essentials for *sustaining* a long marriage?"

When we discuss how we prepared for our marriage we can come up with little historical evidence. I still have the letter describing how Roger designed and ordered our bed. It is unique and we still sleep in it so it was well worth the careful planning.

We had the usual talk with our friend Ted Wickham, who was to perform the marriage ceremony. The only thing I can remember about that occasion was that he told us, smiling from ear to ear, that if we reversed the drive band on our vacuum cleaner we could blow the fallen leaves into our neighbour's garden. Useful information in the leafy suburb of Sheffield where we had just bought our first house.

My mother did not give me any advice as she was not the advice-giving sort, and what I knew about housekeeping came from observation and a term at a "finishing school" where we learned basic cookery and made a set of underwear, by hand, French knickers with a scalloped hem handsewn. The unspoken assumption was that they were for our trousseau. And of course we learned mending, that lost art. How irrelevant it feels in 2006, except as social history, but the questions asked above show that we have moved from assuming marriage will be for life to wondering whether it will be and what can we do to make it so.

When I married I expected to be a homemaker and if I had wanted a career I would not have married. That was true of nearly all my contemporaries. *Quaker Faith and Practice* 22–34 suggests we might have aspirations "to found a colony of heaven", but I felt singularly unsuited to doing so and felt that I had somehow to reconstruct myself to be a person worthy of such a venture. I think I probably shut my eyes and hoped it would be alright but it was a steep learning curve. Mercifully I was surrounded by others who were learning too and I had older mentors who guided me. So perhaps we should be less reticent in offering guidance in an informal way, not only when things go wrong, for, as Roger says, Relate is too late! But responding in a more thoughtful way when asked "How did you do it?", I should try harder to translate what we did in such a different climate into something that can resonate in today's world, rather than feeling we are relics from a past era which cannot be replicated. Erich Fromm's book *The Art of Loving* (1957) contains truths that remain the same for ever, but society needs to support these truths, and that is where we can exert the effort for change.

We expected to be married for life and we learned quickly that it would not all be plain sailing. We know that nowadays children are not on everyone's agenda, nor should they be, but the arrival of our children was a real test. I cannot underline strongly enough the support we shared with our contemporary friends during those early years. All the women were at home, all had husbands who were totally involved in their work and had little time to spare on a day to day basis, so we young wives and mothers were there for each other.

Although the rise of individualism is cited as one of the main reasons why modern marriage is thought to be in such dire straits, the concept of self discovery and the growth of the personal development movement coincided with our move from a situation of maximum support and lifelong friendships, in Sheffield, to one where I knew hardly anyone, in Northampton. So I set forth, on my own, to discover how I operated, with some vague sense that I needed to find out what gave me life. Unexpectedly, this search showed me that one of the chief ingredients of a lifelong relationship was to be able to be alone and value oneself. Marriage is not a panacea for loneliness and getting married to avoid it can trap both partners. I was not so much reconstructing myself, which sounds too much like knocking the whole edifice down and starting again, as looking at what was there in a new light and moving on from there to somewhere that was, I hoped, to the advantage of us both.

Synergy

Marriage is bigger than we are, a vocation, into which we have been drawn by nature and by God.

Quaker Faith and Practice 22.41

. . . The binding business of life on the hard earth, in which one is exorably aware of the otherness of the other . . .

Martin Buber (1947 p.32)

Sitting in our favourite taverna, we were considering how we should respond to the Swarthmore Lecture committee's suggestion that we write and speak about a "Long Marriage". We felt it was only worth doing if we could demonstrate that the merger of two such different personalities, working together in marriage, had been more productive than the sum of our individual efforts. We were groping round for the word that conveyed this when we spied a man with a T-shirt saying "Cambridge University" and consulted him. He did not know but his wife did . . . "Synergy", appropriately a teaching of the Eastern Orthodox church that God and human beings co-operate in grace and liberty . . . synergism.

At the beginning of the project I was walking through the National Gallery when my eye was caught by a portrait of an elderly man and woman side by side gazing morosely into the distance. It was titled "An Elderly Couple" by the 16th century painter Jan Gossaert, and I said to my companion, "If we end up looking like that it is not worth it!" Hopefully we look a little more engaged?

Our contention is that a lifelong relationship is the best framework for learning "The Art of Loving", the title Erich Fromm gave to his influential book. In a loving relationship we learn to overcome our natural tendency to see the world and others from a self-centred point of view, so that we can learn to care for them and respect them in tandem with learning to love and care for ourselves. As Mary Grey suggests, "moving out of the living patterns of the 'enclosed I' of modernity and recovering the relational and connected" (Grey 1997 p.36).

There is a beautiful Xhosa word, beloved of Nelson Mandela, "Ubuntu". "I am what I am because I exist in relationship to you". At the beginning of the 21st century marriage has become a contract between individuals and is no longer seen as the way in which communities renew themselves through the creation of new life and new energy for life. In contrast we need to have faith that the synergy created within marriage will flow out into the world and that in God we have the power to make right relationships.

4 Marriage – Roger

Catalysts? How Then Shall We Live?

We were married on 14 September 1957 at the parish church at Little
Aston near Birmingham, where Susan's parents lived. We had bought
a spacious Victorian house in Sheffield a few weeks earlier and had a
party there for our Sheffield friends who could not get to the wedding.
We were not living together before we married, this would have been
scandalous in middle-class Sheffield at the time, and even the party at
our future home was seen as rather improper. We imported strawberries
from the continent and champagne, but it was not a wild occasion and
there was certainly no binge drinking or riotous stag party.

We were both active in church organisations so it was an overtly
Christian wedding. Ted Wickham,* our friend and mentor, married
us, assisted by another friend, Raymond Bailey, an early member of
the Iona Community. We had no discernment at that time that radical
approaches to industrial organisation or community living would be
important concerns of our life together. Perhaps Ted did have some
such discernment because he refused to preach what he dismissively
termed a "luvvy-duvvy, moon-June" marriage homily but, instead,
charged us to be "catalysts", choosing a word used in the chemistry of
steelmaking, a substance which causes change but is neither consumed
nor weakened by such change.

Catalyst is a word which has remained with us ever since,
particularly when we have felt overwhelmed by the changes going on
around us, both at home and at work.

A Committed Lifelong Loving Relationship

These are big words but what do they mean in our context? What is
commitment if there is no legal bond and how do we define a loving
relationship except by the negative device of excluding marriages

* E.R. Wickham. Leader of the Sheffield Industrial Mission 1944–59, Bishop of
Middleton 1959–82. For biography see Bloy 2000.

of convenience, like some asylum seekers or historical monarchs or wealthy people concerned about inheritance? And we have deliberately used the word "lifelong" rather than "longterm" or "permanent", because, for the purposes of this writing, marriage is considered a lifelong bond, "till death us do part".

We acknowledge, of course, that separation and divorce are widespread and, in our view, sometimes justified as the better of two bad alternatives. Our son is divorced but his three sisters are all married, by our definition. Our closest neighbour is separated after eighteen years marriage and we know something of the pain of such fractured relationships and broken promises. However, we choose to use the word marriage to include all those who set out with the honest intention of a lifelong partnership, rather than "let's just see how long we want to stay together".

So what is "love" in the context of marriage and what is a loving relationship? Armfuls of books, shelves of poetry, countless plays have been written to answer such a vital but elusive question. For example, Paul the apostle to the gentiles, writing his letter to the young church at Corinth in the early 50s CE, contributes the wonderful chapter about love and says that it can hardly be expressed in words:

> If I speak in the tongues of mortals and angels but do not
> have love, I am a noisy gong. . . . love is patient . . . endures all
> things. Love never ends . . . (1 Corinthians 13:1 NRSV)

Over a thousand years later, Shakespeare has several goes at defining love, perhaps more earthy and less ethereal than Paul:

> Let me not to the marriage of true minds
> Admit impediments. Love is not love
> Which alters when it alteration finds
> Or bends with the remover to remove:
> O, no! it is an ever-fixed mark . . . (Sonnet 116)

It is clear that neither the apostle nor the bard are writing of short-term or easily terminated partnerships. These two, among the most influential writers of all time, are describing longterm if not lifelong relationships in which "love never ends" and "bears it out", the "star to every wandering barque". We can count on both of them as allies for marriage as a hoped-for lifelong commitment.

At the risk of being woefully inadequate or hopelessly misunderstood, we offer the following objectives of our marriage. These are no more than characteristics. They are not intended to be definitive nor comprehensive and we have often failed to maintain them, but hopefully they point us in the direction we want to go. You, our reader, may wish to subtract or add to them from your own experience.

What characterises a lifelong loving relationship?

- It is safekeeping. At marriage there is a sense in which we each hand over our lives to the other for safekeeping. Each of us becomes responsible not only for our own life but also for the life of our partner. We support each other emotionally and defend each other against the perils which may beset us.
- It is confidentiality, a secure place in which to share experiences and feelings, trusting one another with knowledge that we may not impart to anyone else, not even our best friend or closest relative.
- It is sexual attraction, wanting "to make love" rather than just "to have sex".
- It is forgiveness, not bearing grudges against each other nor seeking revenge.
- In a faith-based marriage, it is worshipping together.
- It is trusting each other about money, putting all our income into a single pot rather than two separate pots, and leaving everything to each other in our wills.
- It is caring at times of sickness, feeding, washing, practical everyday caring freely given, when one partner is weak, vulnerable, fragile and at risk of depression.

Marriage Critics? – The Apostle Paul & George Fox

As long-married people gathering the arguments in favour of marriage, both for this book and for justification, we need also to look at the arguments against.

Somewhat to our consternation they are several and powerful. For example, the apostle Paul, whatever our view of him, has been one of the most influential teachers of the last two thousand years and both Acts and his letters to young churches continue to be widely read by Christians and by seekers all over the world. In his first letter to the Corinthians he devotes a whole chapter to marriage and, at first reading, appears to be against it, so that he is often thought of as a killjoy by Bible readers. To the unmarried, he suggests they stay unmarried and continue to live alone as he did. Widows will be happiest if they do not remarry (1 Corinthians 7:8–9). However, on closer study and in the context of the whole chapter, perhaps he is a realist rather than a spoiler because, along with many of the early Christians, Paul believed the world as they knew it would shortly come to an end, Jesus would return and the Kingdom of God would be inaugurated.

Although he was wrong about the timing, and might be surprised that the same old world is still turning in 2006, there have always been people predicting the end of the world, whether with sandwich boards, "PREPARE TO MEET THY DOOM", or after disasters like the Krakatoa eruption in 1883, the most earth-shattering event in recorded history. So in the eschatological setting of his time, Paul tells the Corinthians to concentrate their actions on the expected cataclysmic expectations of the Second Coming and not be diverted by materialistic problems and worldly liaisons such as marriage.

However, he then softens his argument a little with the often-quoted and misquoted line, "it is better to marry than to be aflame with passion". Burning is destructive, and Paul's view is that unrequited passion can be destructive, so rather than taking the risk of being "destroyed" by remaining single, it is better to take the next worst option and get married. Grin and bear it! But recollect that he was not preaching but replying in writing to specific questions put to him by the new Christians in Corinth whose lives were being turned upside down by their conversion.

Paul then quotes Jesus, of recent memory because he is writing only twenty years after the Crucifixion. Jesus said that those who do marry should not separate but, if they do separate, should remain single (Matthew 19:9, *TFG* p.219).* Here again Paul is writing in the expectation that the world would soon end and if he was here today perhaps he would agree with us that hopelessly unhappy married couples should not continue indefinitely in a destructive relationship. He writes, "those who marry will experience distress in this life and I would spare you that" (1 Corinthians 7:28). Not very encouraging to newly-weds but Paul knew that in his day marriage problems could have disastrous consequences because the contract was taken very seriously. Under Mosaic law, adultery could be punished by death.

It was Jesus who put forward a totally counter-cultural view. The woman "caught in the very act of adultery" would have been stoned to death if Jesus had not intervened, after a period of silence, with his devastating comment, "whoever is sinless in this crowd should go ahead and throw the first stone at her" (John 8:4–7, *TFG* p.425). No wonder he was so unpopular with the Pharisees who were intent on upholding the Law. Hypocrisy is less easy to prove than adultery but Jesus clearly regarded it as just as sinful.

Paul remained single because his gift was to be a writer and a travelling preacher who knew that he risked imprisonment and was indeed imprisoned on several occasions. He had the courage of his convictions but such a life was not one to impose on a wife who would have had few opportunities to earn her own living while her husband was languishing in jail many miles away.

This cautious view is also reflected in the marriage service in the Book of Common Prayer (1662) under which millions of people have been married and many still are despite the availability of more recent Christian marriage liturgies. The prayer book service states that marriage should not be undertaken "unadvisedly, lightly or wantonly" and, even more threatening to people joyfully preparing to get married, it tells us that marriage was ordained "to avoid fornication" among "such persons as have not the gift of continency". The inference here is that those who do have the gift of continency may be well-

---

* The Gospels include several sayings of Jesus about divorce and they differ slightly from each other so that there is some doubt about his authentic words. However, there is no doubt that he regarded marriage as a serious undertaking and regretted any departure from it.

advised not to marry at all. Perhaps the authors of this solemn warning were unmarried, like Paul, and anxious to justify such celibacy.

Sixteen hundred years after Paul, George Fox, another influential writer and itinerant preacher, says: "For the right joining in marriage is the work of the Lord only, not the priests or the magistrates . . . we marry none; it is the Lord's work and we are but witnesses" (*QFP* 16.01). *Quaker Faith & Practice* Chapter 16 devotes twenty nine pages and fifty six paragraphs to marriage which is an indication of the importance which Quakers have attached to it over the years. The following chapter, on Quaker funerals and memorial meetings, is only eight pages.

Fox declared that marriage must be a spiritual union and not just a worldly legal contract and there were restrictions which limited Friends to "marrying-in" to other Friends, to preserve the testimonies. This restriction seems to have caused the Society to become rather in-bred and it was not rescinded until 1859, two hundred years after the foundation. Thereafter "marrying-out" does not cause the Quaker partner to be deprived of membership. Some argue that this has led to a dilution of Quaker faith and practice because these "outside" spouses have led their Quaker partners away from Fox's uncompromisingly Christocentric faith, sometimes towards what is now designated a "universalist" position.* In contrast, others argue that marrying-out enhances the Society by bringing new people into the Quaker orbit by way of their marriage rather than by independent "convincement". Many will have become members by this route and others, like myself, have benefited greatly from living alongside a Friend and being in touch with the peculiarities of the Society. Whatever the resolution of this debate, marrying-out has certainly changed the make-up of Quaker meetings and we discuss this further in Chapter 5, "A Quaker Married to a Non-Quaker".

* "Universalism" is an ambivalent word. In mainstream Christian theology it is defined as "the doctrine that all mankind will eventually be saved" (*OED*). However, during the last century Friends have extended the meaning of "universalist" to categorise those who give prominence to various spiritual paths, not only Christianity. With this latter meaning, many Christians regard themselves as universalists and some Friends, describing themselves as universalists, are also Christians in that they accept the divinity of Christ. See *QFP* 27.04.

Marriage Vows

The assumption at the time of our wedding was that if one got married, particularly in church, then one stayed married and coped with any difficulties which might arise.

We were not naïve, we were aged thirty and twenty five, had travelled and worked in different situations, had plenty of friends who were married. We knew that the picture of married bliss, social poise and perfectly arranged dinner parties, as peddled by the glossy magazines, was not the lifestyle to which we aspired. Our sights were set at a lower social level, one which we thought we could cope with. In 1957 we knew only a few people who were separated or divorced and were probably dismayed that they found it possible to dispense with their marriage vows. Certainly we accepted without question that our marriage was for life and it was a joyful occasion to make our promises of love and fidelity in front of many witnesses, family and friends, in church. If we had known about it, we would have welcomed the beautiful Quaker practice of all present signing the specially decorated Certificate of Marriage, a symbol and reminder of such a significant occasion. It would have taken pride of place on the wall of our living room.

We can recall no hesitation in saying "for better, for worse, till death us do part". Beforehand, Susan hesitated over "obey" but allowed herself to be persuaded by Ted Wickham who held a more traditional view of marriage. He would have a much harder task to persuade her today!

Neither of us considered that we could put our marriage aside if it became inconvenient. Separation or divorce were spoken of in whispers and regarded as shameful failure. Our life together has been full of joys but it would be hypocritical to claim that it has been uninterrupted bliss and the vow of fidelity is valuable when facing times of contrary views. The fundamental agreement that we will not walk away from our relationship is a form of freedom, not imprisonment or servitude. There will be several options to solving a situation of disagreement but separation is not one of them. Although neither of us had read it at the time of our wedding, we would have united, and still do, with *Advices and Queries* 23, "Marriage has always been regarded by Friends as a religious commitment rather than a merely civil contract."

This view would have been acceptable to many in 1957, Friends or not, but in the fifty years at which we are looking, the culture has changed to one in which, if a relationship becomes difficult, one can walk away from it without excessive feelings of guilt or shame. Separation is no longer regarded as unusual nor is the same stigma attached to the discontinuity of marriage vows, although I suspect that this view is sometimes transmitted by fluent writers and speakers for their own ends and may not represent the view of the more silent majority. Posy Simmonds' cartoon *Why Marriage?* on page 50 neatly summarises the huge changes in the culture of marriage which have occurred during the span of our marriage. Our expectations in 1957 were vastly different from those now getting married in the 21st century. Now serial marrying has become popular in the USA and perhaps is now spreading to the UK. We know of more than one recent Quaker marriage which has been short-lived and caused great unhappiness and we have been surprised that Quakers, who put such weight on truth that they choose to affirm rather than "swear on the Bible" in a courtroom, have been able to forego their marriage vows so soon (see *Advices and Queries* 25).

The reasons for the change of culture are several and not hard to find. They include the new-found ability of single women to earn their own living, the increasing reliability of birth control, and the cult of the individual rather than mutuality. These developments, endlessly debated, have led to legislation which is hard for older people to believe, let alone put into practice. For example, a provisional divorce, decree nisi, may now be obtained on-line. Computer-literate people can provisionally reverse out of their marriage by pressing a few keys and by so doing, dispense with the expense and possible arguments of the divorce court (see an article by Mary Riddell, "See you in court", in the *New Statesman*, 29 November 2004). Such changes may prove healthy if they diminish the number of distressed marriages in which one or both, but particularly women, feel trapped and unable to escape because of the problems of earning a living or the moral pressure of friends, colleagues and family. Where there is near or total breakdown then surely separation is no less moral than living with the joyless energy-sapping hypocrisy of a marriage which is broken but attempts to maintain the appearance of being unbroken?

Nevertheless we must avoid diluting marriage too far. Sadness and a sense of failure are almost inevitable in a separation and the change of culture has an unhealthy component if it encourages couples to avoid marriage because of the risk of failure, or to avoid the obligations of marriage, or worse still, to assume there are no obligations worth bothering about.

Marriage and Money

Some people enjoy discussing personal income and spending patterns, others find it embarrassing or even unacceptable, one of the last taboos and therefore to be avoided at all costs. We all need money and use it, so whether articulated or not, the spending of it becomes an outward and visible sign of our priorities, noticed by those around us as well as ourselves. In this way money has the useful function of affirming our integrity or showing up our hypocrisy. On several occasions, Jesus condemns hypocrisy and appears to regard it as a significant missing of the mark, in contrast to the more easily recognised sins such as dishonesty or adultery. He questions the decision to stone to death the woman caught in adultery and reserves his severest condemnation for the hypocrisy of the Pharisees. "Damn you!" he says, "you are like whitewashed tombs," graves disguised as something else (Matthew 23:27, *TFG* p.243).

Regarding the right use of money, we note, with some alarm, that those like ourselves who preach charity are not necessarily more charitable in our giving than those who say little but give more. Money is a relentless measure of what we regard as important and this includes the way we pay our debts for services rendered, as mundane as the gas bill or as flamboyant as buying flowers for the person we love.

Money is also a measure of our relationships with other people including, of course, the marriage relationship. The way we deal with money within the marriage strengthens or weakens the committed loving relationship to which we aspire. So what can we say? As an expression of mutual trust we put all our income, from whatever source, into one common pot and then decide between us what to do with it. At first glance this may seem the same as each having our own individual bank accounts and deciding who pays for what, but there is a real philosophical difference between these two procedures, and it matters. Once the principle is established that the money in the pot is jointly owned, we give up our personal claim to it and cannot retrieve it. "My earnings" or "your travel expenses" become "our income" when they both go into the same bank account. This may seem obvious but we were surprised to note a survey in the *Guardian* ("Nothing is sacred in love and bank statements", 5 April 2005) which claimed that a significant proportion of "people in relationships" did not regard sharing information about their finances as important, let alone having a shared bank account. The report comments: "There is increasing potential for relationships to founder on lack of trust. People can be tied together financially without knowing that much about each other's finances."

Our finances have varied considerably during the half century of our marriage. In the early years, I was the sole breadwinner, earning a comfortable salary in the steel industry which enabled us to buy our first house without a mortgage and run a car each together with a motor caravan for holidays. Susan discontinued her paid work as an occupational therapist and was soon fully occupied with raising the children, the conventional pattern at that time when working wives were the exception rather the rule. This material "dreamworld" of ongoing financial security was shattered in an ironic fashion when I was offered the key job as Managing Director of Spear & Jackson, the position at which I had been aiming for fifteen years. I responded to the offer from the Board of Directors by saying I would be glad to do the job, wanted to do it, but before accepting I would like to be sure I had their support in moving the company away from the paternalistic management style and introducing some procedures for involving more people, at all levels, in the decision-making process. Such ideas were radical and controversial at that time and it was my heaven-sent opportunity to put into practice the thoughts that had been swirling round in my head for some years. My colleagues, including the Chairman, said no, this was too risky and they saw little reason to change the style that had kept the company in prosperity for two hundred years.* Angry and sulky, I gave in my notice and left without having any idea what to do next – and we had four small children.

* In due course, Spear & Jackson, founded in 1760, fell into financial difficulties in the 1980s and suffered the humiliation of being taken over, first by a rival Sheffield tool maunufacturer and then, horror of horrors, by a faceless merchant bank.

With the benefit of hindsight, was this taking a risk under guidance, because unexpected doors began to open? We decided to go travelling, all six of us in our motor caravan, overland to Israel, not only to fulfil a long-held eagerness to visit the Holy Land, but also to try living on a kibbutz. When we arrived, after three months and many travelling adventures, I was invited to work in the kibbutz factory making engineers' tools. There I experienced for the first time a democratic co-operative work structure and, on returning to the UK, searched for a similar opportunity by conducting a substantial survey of companies operating participative decision-making schemes.* This survey led me to Wollaston near Northampton, where a substantial Quaker-influenced chemical company, Scott Bader, offered the lease of an old shoe factory as an opportunity to develop a new employee-owned business. This was the opportunity, so in 1968 we moved to Northampton and I hurled myself into this counter-cultural work at Trylon Ltd at a much-reduced salary, decided upon by the working group. Susan returned to paid work when the children were all school age.

Arriving in Northampton, we reduced from three cars to a small green van and from a spacious Victorian house to a more compact one at a time when numbers of our friends were moving up the housing ladder. We never felt materially deprived because we had not been extravagant spenders but, inevitably, the children wailed that "everyone" had more pocket money than they did. "Why can't you be a solicitor or a doctor or a bank manager, Dad, like most of my friends? It's so embarrassing." We needed to make social changes, also, because we moved from a large city where we were known and accepted to a town where we knew no one and where incomers were viewed with some suspicion. As a Magistrate in Sheffield, Roger was transferred to the Northampton bench but they were somewhat hesitant to accept a "young stranger", who was not even a country landowner or a retired colonel. He was also a Freeman of the Cutlers' Company, the ancient and influential livery company of the steel industry, with the

* *Sharing Our Industrial Future* (The Industrial Society 1968) was sponsored by William Temple College, Rugby. The Steering Committee for the book was chaired by the Earl of March, Director of Industrial Studies at the College, and included Adrian Cadbury, then Chairman of Cadbury Brothers Ltd.

expectation that he would become Master Cutler in due course and he was well-established at the best cricket and squash club in Sheffield, where his father had been a founder member.

Many wives would have basked in this social sunshine and the opportunities it provided, but Susan's concerns were not with such socialising. She had no wish to be Mistress Cutler, opening church bazaars, and her ideas were more concerned with the kind of social justice which had motivated both her grandfather in Derby and her father when he was a Labour MP. In Northampton she had no standing in the local community, four demanding children and a husband who seemed to be always at work. It was not even the sort of work which brought much immediate income nor the deferred rewards which often hold conventional entrepreneurs to their course.

After this move in 1968, we both worked for about twenty five years before retiring with our State Pensions but no pension from employment. In Sheffield we had been able to put aside some savings towards our old age and this has been of great benefit to us more recently, but saving was no longer possible in Northampton. Providentially at this time, Roger's parents left us a small legacy, and Susan's a larger one later, although by then the children had grown up and our outgoings were less. In retrospect, there were times when our expenditure exceeded our income for years on end and we had to dip into our savings to make ends meet, but we have never been impoverished by debt nor embarrassed by riches.

More recently, influenced by the Quaker testimony of simplicity and frugality, we have tried to decide on a right ordering of expenditure, quite independent of current income or the lack of it. The downside result of this procedure of deliberately breaking the customary link between income and expenditure, has sometimes touched on meanness and a tendency for Roger to spend undue time on adding up figures or projecting our financial future. Our stance has been one of old-fashioned caution rather than improvident spending and we realise now that this is partly inherited from our parents, three of whom endured times of real impoverishment when they were young. Susan's father was the only one of the four who did not have money problems.

We made decisions which may have seemed unreasonably

frugal to our peers and certainly to our children who claimed they were seldom allowed to buy ice cream, even on holiday. Later on we relented a little as we were influenced by the experience of Jack Bellerby, an elderly friend who, as a gifted young academic, was Professor of Economics at Liverpool University in the 1930s but decided that it was his Christian vocation to give up the glittering prizes of his academic career, resign his professorship and live on the average wage of the time, about £2 per week, in a tumbledown cottage in Cornwall. After some years he abandoned the project, not because of material impoverishment but because his inability to afford books, visit friends or go to the theatre, caused him to be on the edge of depression and incapable of "being there for others". Subsistence living had absorbed all his energies, mental and spiritual as well as physical. Jack related this to us fifty years afterwards and, learning from his experience, we have not hesitated to spend money on maintaining friendships, travel and recreation to avoid burnout. This was not "living for holidays" but seeking a balance between work and recreation, a delicate balance which can easily tip too much one way or the other. Love of money may well be the root of all evil but, without becoming too attached, a sufficiency of money can also be the means of much joy and fulfilment.

During these various changes of financial circumstances, we paid all our income, from whatever source, into our joint bank account with which either of us can sign cheques, independent of the other. There has been one exception, lest this sounds too idealistic. When a much-loved aunt left Susan a small legacy, she put it into a separate account "for luxuries in memory of Aunty Catherine" and for what she called her "running away fund", although it would not have taken her much further than Crewe. It was a bid to have some money for the spending of which she need not reach mutual agreement. When the legacy was spent, we closed the account and continued to use the joint account only. But we now have a large number of CDs and enjoy them.

Children

If there are children of the marriage, vowed or unvowed, then a stable relationship between the two parents will help to provide a secure background against which they can grow up and develop their own views.

Our children and the grandchildren have been a constant joy to us and any reference to grumbles about meanness need to be understood within the wider context of a family that has stayed together. They are all over forty at the time of writing and although they live miles apart, they are frequently in and out of each other's house and have a wonderful arrangement for looking after each other's children to give the parents a break. They all have demanding jobs and occasional child-minding crises. We enjoy our grandparenting role of "holding the fort" from time to time, a singularly inappropriate phrase as none of our children would have voted for the war in Iraq in 2003. We have joined them on peace marches and, on one occasion, surrounding the American Cruise missile base at Molesworth at Easter 1985, we have a picture of a policeman helping children to cross a muddy ditch to get to the perimeter fence.

We hope that they have gained some benefit from our marriage. All four were baptised and came with us to church on Sundays, willingly or reluctantly, as part of the "religious commitment" of our marriage, as mentioned in *Advices and Queries* 23, although it was not until the youngest had grown up that Susan made the significant theological move to join Friends and we both made the equally fundamental change to live in a Christian community of households.

Parents finding themselves in an unstable failing marriage, for whatever reason, have a difficult choice to make. The conventional wisdom when our children were young was that parents stayed together "for the sake of the children". Remaining in an unhappy marriage, being miserable together was considered preferable to being doubly miserable separately. Now, in the 21st century, the culture has changed and separation is not only more widespread but has also lost some of its stigma. However, the practical situation has not changed because whichever parent has the children must also earn a living. This takes time and energy and probably produces less money for bringing up children than staying together would deliver. Few will deny that lone parenting is a difficult role. This is the concluding paragraph of a report for the Maternity Alliance about the experiences and needs of homeless women with babies, in London:

This study is a story of survival against all the odds.
The women lived one day at a time in their dirty, infested
and overcrowded accommodation. They cried as they told
me of their feelings of personal failure and their sense of
hurt that they, and more importantly their children, were
viewed by society as an underclass worthy only of treatment
as a "last step before the street" level. They searched for
explanations as to why they were receiving so little help from
service providers when they felt they had done nothing to
deserve such neglect. But they also told me of their dreams.
They dreamt of a flat somewhere safe and pleasant, near
their friends and family, where their children could grow
up, "be free", be healthy, and go to school . . . These are not
unreasonable dreams . . . (Sawtell 2002).

We do not consider that there is now, or ever has been in our lifetime,
an inviolable case for parents always to stay together in a marriage
fractured by arguments, suspicion and resentment. There are situations
in which a failing marriage provides less stability for the children than
may be provided by a trusted and loving lone parent. So, although it
remains true that children are likely to flourish best if they witness day
to day love and consistency in both their parents, there is sometimes a
valid case for separation if the parents are destroying one another. Jesus'
unchanging law of love takes precedence over subsequent teaching
which may take insufficient account of the huge social and economic
changes which have taken place over the last two thousand years.

Benedict's wisdom has allowed his monasteries to adapt their
Rule without losing the underlying purpose, but there has not been
an equivalent guidebook for parents and children who, of course, lie
outside the monastery walls. Shakespeare says it again in the sonnet
referred to earlier:

Love's not Time's fool, though rosy lips and cheeks
Within his bending sickle's compass come;
Love alters not with his brief hours and weeks,
But bears it out even to the edge of doom.

The balance between the options of staying together or separating may
be hard to find but it needs to be worked out with today's "bending

sickle" and weighing scales rather than accepting an historical edict laid down by a hierarchical church or an outdated law.

Bringing Together Differing Gifts

A justification for a long marriage is that it produces synergy. We discover that the combined energy of two people in a committed relationship is greater than the sum of energy of the same two people unrelated or in an unloving relationship.

Jesus is sometimes described as "the man for others". If we are expending emotional energy on arguing with our partners or scheming to get our own way, we have that much less energy for other people, as envisaged in the Gospels. If we are locked into our own problems and these lead to separation or divorce, there are then two people each burning up energy in anger or resentment and so the energy available for others is depleted. The converse is that the synergy of a stable marriage, one plus one equals three, not two, adds to the energy available.

There is also the partnership of gifts/charisms. One may be an "ideas" person and the other an "action" person, the former having the gift of envisaging a new approach to a problem and the latter having the organisational gift to earth the vision into a working structure. Such complementary gifts are present in any successful partnership, at work or politics or wherever, but they are of particular significance in the marriage relationship, and a cause of much happiness if such differing gifts can be welded together. John, the Gospel writer, expresses it, "so planter and harvester can celebrate together" (John 4:36–7, *TFG* p.411).

In our case, we realise, long after the events took place, that Roger's fundamental work change at age forty, from being a conventional manager in the Sheffield steel industry to becoming an entrepreneur in the counter-cultural field of employee-owned co-operative businesses, would not have happened if we had not been able to share the vision and the practicalities of shaping it, including moving house, uprooting children from schools, and changing our lifestyle. Throughout these years of transformation we needed to make dozens of lifestyle decisions, often one "sowing" and the other "reaping". It was always understood that these were joint decisions and if there had been no synergy, the change from Sheffield to Northampton might have overwhelmed us. Without synergy, this once-in-a-lifetime attempt to be catalysts, as enjoined by Ted Wickham ten years earlier, would have failed ignominiously.

Moreover, if our marriage had ended, say, during Sheffield days, it is unlikely that I would have stepped alone into such insecure territory but would have suppressed my discernment, taken up the lucrative offer to be Managing Director of Spear & Jackson, probably becoming wealthy and possibly world-weary. Correspondingly, Susan might have been "trapped" in the Church of England, busily opening parish bazaars and never making her life-enhancing move to Quakerism.

The year between leaving Spear & Jackson and starting work at Trylon was a crucial time. The well-known and beautiful words in Ecclesiastes (1:12–13 and 3:6–7) "a time to seek and a time to lose . . . a time to tear and a time to sew," were spoken by the philosopher king not in celebration but in disappointment. He was powerful and had accumulated "great possessions" but it all turned out to be shallow and futile, like "chasing the wind". He concluded that God disposes but he could not understand this God who appeared to control human destiny. Ecclesiastes contrasts with the Gospels, written many years later and describing a very different Kingdom. Working towards it need not be chasing the wind because it brings us closer to the transcendent loving God whose Kingdom it is and whose presence we seek, bringing together whatever gifts we have received.

Marriage and Community Living

When I use the word community in this book I am talking essentially of groupings of people who have left their own milieu to live with others under the same roof and work from a new vision of human beings and their relationship with each other and with God.
Jean Vanier (1989 p.10)

The Church in its origins creates considerable tension with the society around because it will not take for granted (even if it will not often challenge head-on) the finality and authority of the socially prevailing accounts of status and power. The more Christianity ceases to be a communal life . . . the more this tension is eroded.
Rowan Williams (in McGrandle 2004)

How then shall we live? For well over twenty years, nearly half our married life, we have lived in a residential community of households,

The Neighbours Community. How has this affected our marriage? What can we say?

Our task, married or not, is to discover a deeper sense of God's presence in our lives. Each of us is a child of God and therefore we are all brothers and sisters and, as we stand in the love of God, we are committed to one another. There is no unique way of living out this commitment and we must each find our own way. There are a number of options.

The contemporary conventional pattern of living is the independent household which may be a single person or two partners or parents with children. The assumption is that each household is independent from the adjoining one and sociologists call this pattern "little boxes". The inmates of each box may chat over the garden fence or borrow a litre of milk from each other but alternatively may choose to have no social contact whatever with next door and may not even know who lives next door, particularly in city flats. It is not unusual for people living alone to be found dead in their own home days or even weeks after they have died.

Many people committed to the search for God's presence in their lives continue to live in an ordinary house in an ordinary street and, to their neighbours, there is little evidence of their searching. All independent households are subject to the pressures the media dream up to encourage us to acquire more possessions and they tell us that a bigger television will bring more happiness and a new kitchen will bring untold joys to the daily tasks of cooking and washing up. Of course they are right, up to a point. Improved household equipment can lift our spirits and cleaning pots and pans with a birch twig is laborious, but the gains are limited and the fundamental search is hardly touched by television or kitchen hardware. This independent lifestyle is adopted, for better or for worse, by well over 90% of the population; the searchers among them will keep the media in their place, resist becoming manic shoppers and never abandon the quest.

There are alternative patterns of living such as monasteries and unvowed communities, which for some will assist the search. They are not obligatory nor even helpful to all searchers but these alternatives do help to maintain the "rightful tension" which Rowan Williams identifies, by challenging the "socially prevailing accounts of status and power".

For example, we have a friend who reached a turning point in his career and searched for the way forward, feeling empty and out of touch with the vision which had led him to the ordained ministry as a young man. Waiting for a train on York station, one of the longest platforms in England, he watched an interminable goods train trundle slowly past him. On every identical truck was a notice, RETURN EMPTY TO SCOTLAND, like a mantra. He realised that this was the call for which he had been waiting and praying, so he did return to Scotland and for over forty years he has lived a simple life in a tin hut which had once been the "miner's welfare". He has no television and the most basic kitchen where the Bible is kept in a breadbin at the end of the kitchen table so that it is easily available for reference. Over this long period of time he has helped many people in their search and his simple and cheerful hospitality is entirely adequate.

Our friend's experience of a relatively solitary life is unusual and another pattern is the convent or monastery in which each person has a cell but all other space is communal, including the dining room, chapel, kitchen and garden. The monks or nuns take vows of celibacy, frugality and obedience, all of which are quite contrary to the television ads which bombard us. The monastic life is lived as a community with a corporate discipline which helps rather than hinders the search for God's presence. For example, the Benedictine Rule initiated in the 6th century CE and continuously adapted to a changing world is founded on the unchanging need for a rhythm of prayer and work which sometimes seem almost interchangeable. The prayer is the work, said Benedict, and the monks sometimes answer that the work is the prayer. However one defines the two words, work and prayer, the daily pattern of prayer in chapel and manual work in house or field, it is a way of conducting the search that has been fruitful for fifteen hundred years. How else can its continuity be explained?

These two patterns of living, independent household and monastic, are so disparate that it is not surprising that many Christians have felt uncomfortable that the search, the response to the Gospel, can only be conducted in one or the other. So there have always been experiments with alternative arrangements of bricks and mortar which underpin the unchanging commitment to love our neighbour

as well as ourselves. For example, during the early years of our
marriage in the 1960s, there were numerous "communes", some secular
some Christian, in which young people lived as a community with
much space in common but without the austerity or the longterm
vows which are fundamental to the monastic orders. Some such
communes continue (the directory *Diggers and Dreamers* describes
ninety communities) but most of the 1960s ones have disappeared;
some failed to agree on the ideological focus of the community, be it
sustainability or Buddhist or Christian or other, and some foundered
on the rocks encountered when incorporating children into a
communal structure. It is one thing to be twenty and single, living
in such a community, but at thirty five, perhaps with a partner and
children, it is quite a different social dynamic. Communes are seldom
associated with celibacy.

Another pattern is what we term a "community of households".
This is not a commune because each household has its own front door,
kitchen and living room, nor is it a monastery because the members
are unvowed lay people.

There are many variations, such as a large house split up into
separate units for families or single people. Alternatively, community
members may live in separate houses but near or adjoining each other
in the same street. The essential characteristics of a community of
households are that the members live near enough to each other to
meet daily and that each household is in a committed relationship with
the other households. This commitment may be in terms of economic
sharing of lawn mowers, washing machines or cars and sharing of
some meals. In the case of Christian communities, the commitment is
to meet daily for worship. This pattern may seem new or unexplored
but perhaps it is truer to say that it was the pattern of the early church
in Jerusalem, long before there were any Christian church buildings.
Luke comments, "day by day they spent much time together . . . from
house to house" (Acts 2:46; see also Philemon 2, "the church in your
house"). This is the pattern of living which we have been exploring,
developing, struggling with, for a quarter of a century. At times
despairing of ourselves or our brothers and sisters in the Community,
we have wrung our hands and said we are deceiving ourselves if we
think that by living in this way we have distanced ourselves from the

temptations of selfishness or the false dawns of consumerism. But at other times we are lifted by some decision or action which indicates that community living is indeed a valuable way of conducting the search. Within the churches at the time of writing there is little evidence that Christians are concerned with Rowan Williams' call for a "distinctive community life" but there are some signs of it in the stories of lay residential communities which are both "distinctive" and "communal". We celebrate this and pass on the experience to others looking for a way.

For Susan and me, community living has led to a more disciplined prayer life because corporate morning prayers are an obligation which we both accept and the discipline of a group is sometimes stronger than the discipline of a married couple, living as a lone household. To be a member of this Community commits us to being at prayers and to being part of the decision-making associated with it. Although it is quite possible, of course, for a married couple to read the Bible together or pray together every day, we never managed to do so on a regular and continuing basis in the twenty seven years of marriage before we joined The Neighbours Community. So if prayer is at the heart of life then living in community can be helpful for lay people in a similar but less demanding manner than a monastic community for celibates.

Also we have found that the support of the Community has enabled us to take on tasks which we would have found impossible as a married couple living independently. In the same way that there is a synergy in marriage itself, there is also a synergy in community living. In our case, providing supportive accommodation for people recovering from mental illness was something we both wanted to do but would have found overwhelming as an independent household. The Community gave us the opportunity to do this for ten years, 1984–1994, because the group of us, helping each other also helped to absorb the stresses of living alongside people struggling to regain health after spending time in a psychiatric hospital. L'Arche houses are high profile examples of this synergy and their founder, Jean Vanier, comments that the assistants have as much to gain as the members who are people with learning disabilities.

At the time of writing, The Neighbours Community has discontinued this specific concern for people with mental health problems and has a rather different focus which is closely concerned with marriage. The Community at present consists of seven adult members and eight sons and daughters of members, aged nine to twenty three. Of the seven members, six have direct experience of marriage; one is a widow, one is separated and there are two married couples. One of the married couples separated for a short time but have been together again during their time with the Community, the other couple is us. Thus within this small community of households, we have a considerable and varied experience of marriage with its blessings, problems and uncertainties. Though rarely voiced at Community meetings, we accept that one of our collective tasks, consciously or unconsciously, is to help the married to stay married and support the unmarried in finding a balance between living alone and living in a residential community. This is more than the neighbourliness which may be found in any street, because we live more closely together. For example, although we have our own front door, we share a staircase and an airing cupboard with "next door" and all of us are in and out of each other's houses more frequently and more spontaneously than conventional neighbours. Some see this as a positive gain as it diminishes isolation but others, especially those who tend to be introverts rather than extraverts, find it uncomfortably intrusive, alright for students living in chaotic rented houses but unacceptable for married couples and children. Protection of space has often been a discussion topic at Community meetings and, inevitably, we have yielded some privacy or intimacy with more open doors than is the case with separate houses.

It is impossible to say whether community living has enhanced or diminished our marriage but we do not regret having set our hands to the task of developing a community of households in 1984 and continuing it to the present day.

❡ *Susan writes . . .*

There have been few times in our marriage when we have lived alone, just the two of us. For the first ten months until our first child was born and from then on a variety of people lived alongside us and I suppose we unconsciously developed coping strategies. We had both been at boarding school, so as a friend who was at Eton said, "It is a good preparation for life together!" We were used to sharing our space. You don't get much privacy with four children. When we set up The Neighbours Community we were clear that each family needed its own front door and we have always been mindful of this, knocking and loudly making our presence known as we enter each other's space. This seems particularly important where there are teenage children who don't want other people barging into their family home and I have had to relearn the ways of being aware of how my presence is impinging on their lives; enough contact to acknowledge their personhood and not too much to presume more than a tentative relationship unless they make the first move. But we are useful when there are emergencies, a power cut can build bridges!

Although we share stairs with the flat next door, on the whole this only causes minor irritations. The current occupant does not like things "filed" on the stairs as he might fall over them. When he is away I have an orgy of placing things on every step. The original occupant of the flat was an elderly person who liked to keep an eye on us and would appear at my side remarking that she liked to see me sitting down in the morning, a luxury which had never been part of her hard working life. She also expected me to be a weather forecaster and this drove me mad and once caused me to beat my fists on the door, shrieking that she knew as much about the weather as I did. But these minor irritations are not a necessary ingredient of community life or, now I come to think of it, perhaps they are. It is not the great questions that divide us but the daily business of bearing with one another. We operate a system of rotas, in which each person is an independent unit, so for the married couples each job comes around twice, two breakfasts on Saturdays, two Thursday evening meals. We are not so liberated that Roger can produce a meal for seven people, although he is good at breakfast if I make the porridge! I have to work hard at feeling generous about this.

I have hardly experienced life alone. Life in relationship is what I have had in abundance, and the interdependence that this brings, which is a balancing act, developing the abilities needed for independence while keeping the openness to our interdependence, of which I become more conscious as each year goes by. Of course there are times when the whole thing becomes too much but mercifully this feeling seems to hit us at different times. What drives one of us to demand instant exit from the community the other deals with quite calmly. It is because our responses to the same situation can be so different that we can create some balance. However the core of what keeps us here is the same, the challenge of creating a worshipping community offering some patterns of worship which others can share.

¶ *Roger writes . . .*

Making Good Marriages Better

Friends are positive about marriage, regarding it as a solemn and happy commitment and far more than just a legal contract. There is joy at the Meeting House when a wedding takes place and such weddings are attended by enthusiastic Friends, not as guests clutching silver invitations, but as members of the Meeting to which the couple belong or may join. This welcome is made explicit in the communal signing of the Marriage Certificate, a custom which we have not found in any other denomination. Although it is sometimes difficult to fill positions such as clerk or treasurer to a Quaker meeting, it appears that the post of registrar of marriages is a popular one and holders do not relinquish it easily, some continuing until they are so old that they can hardly sign their own name!

During the writing of this book we have found that married people, Friends or not, have been very willing to talk about their marriages, sometimes in considerable depth. Despite the high failure rate, it seems that married people continue to like the idea of being married and recent figures show that two out of every five weddings include at least one person who has been married before. Gluttons for punishment or wiser by experience, they decide to "try again", for better for worse, for richer for poorer? In view of this continuing concern for the married state as contrasted with the unvowed relationship, it is surprising that there is no grouping within the Society of Friends specifically for discussing or enhancing marriage. Relate, and other organisations, are concerned with helping to hold fragile relationships together and this is a valuable task; but we have something different in mind, a means of enhancing and consolidating stable marriages in order to increase the synergy. This could be a straightforward discussion group but a better approach, in our view, would be for three married couples, six people, to agree to meet and talk to each other on a regular ongoing basis, say once a month for six months, specifically about their marriages. Subjects would be many and varied and ones that come to mind immediately, for Friends and other faith-based marriages, include:

- Who does what? Sharing out the obligatory tasks
- Spiritual journey as a couple. Praying/worshipping together
- How do we make decisions? Especially where there are differences of opinion
- Sex
- Spending, giving, budgeting of money

This arrangement, which we call "marriage accompaniment", is similar to spiritual accompaniment but in a group of six rather than one to one, and, with Friends' sensibilities in mind, without the hierarchical element implied in the more common term "spiritual direction".

5 A Quaker Married to a Non-Quaker

Single Quaker In Family (SQUIF)

And if any woman has a husband who is an unbeliever, and he
consents to live with her, she should not divorce him. For the
unbelieving husband is made holy through his wife, and the
unbelieving wife is made holy through her husband.
1 Corinthians 7:13–14

§ *Susan writes . . .*

General Meeting had over-run the proposed finishing time but an
assumption was made that Friends would be happy to complete the
programme. I complained to my neighbour that I had had enough and
just wanted to go home. "That is the best thing I've heard all day," she
replied with great emotion. She had come to General Meeting with her
husband, who had recently joined the Society and was so absorbed by
Quaker activities that she only got to spend time with him if she came
too. I wondered how many others were in her situation, unwillingly
trailing round Quaker events. How can we know, when our partners
join something that sounds so benign as the Society of Friends, that it
will take over their whole life?

A well-known Quaker historian remarked that he felt that any
difficulties arising from a Quaker married to a non-Quaker had to
do with the relationship and not the membership. However, if the
relationship is in trouble, membership of what can be a very absorbing
and demanding organisation certainly does not help. Stepping over
the threshold into membership brings demands which non-Quakers
find it hard to appreciate. Anglican friends of ours, well versed in the
ecumenical scene, are amazed at the amount of time given to keeping
the Society going, as they come from a situation where the bottom line
is that someone else is paid to do the jobs Quakers do for themselves
in local meetings. For better or for worse, and often it is for worse, this
someone else is paid to make decisions that we so torturously come to
through our bewildering structures.

Friends who have been long in membership, come from a Quaker family, or have a Quaker partner, seem to lose sight of the non-Quaker perspective that our ways are not understood and sometimes not appreciated. Not everyone subscribes to the theory that "Quakers are such good people". Some of those we employ, or tangle with in our ways of doing business, are less than tolerant of our peculiarities. "Do Quakers think they are the only group who are opposed to war?" grumbled one exasperated ecumenical officer as the Quaker representative banged the peace drum yet again.

For those of us who are "babes in the Society" as one longtime Friend described me, the juggling required to fulfil our role as fully participating members without abandoning our partners for the entire weekend and several evenings in the week, can be a bit of a trial, especially if the clerk of a meeting has a lifetime of service to the Society and their partner likewise. The fact that there are other things to do with a Sunday afternoon rather than ploughing through an immense agenda never seems to strike them. "What could be more important?" they ask.

Fortunately Roger rarely complains, knowing that in his life "the Lord's work" has been equally time consuming. It is me that feels guilty. He is equally generous about giving money to Quaker causes, which can be a bone of contention. Christian Aid or Quaker Peace & Social Witness?

As indicated earlier, the community of the Anglican congregation was vital to me during the early child-rearing years, when Roger's allegiances were to work, the Industrial Mission and our parish church a poor third. But such was the support of my friends, married to clergymen and so in the "married lone parent" position too, that although I may have wished Roger was with me, I felt supported, as did the Quaker married to a non-Quaker, with whom I discussed this. For example, in a Quaker/Roman Catholic marriage, wanting their children to be part of their faith community, or indeed both communities, Mass might be followed by Children's Meeting, poor dears! This may be burdensome for children but if they sometimes attend the worship and the social events of both congregations, at least they experience the difficulties with which their parents are living, even if Sunday lunch is a non-event. In due course they are able to make their own informed choice.

I am glad I am not entirely lodged in one religious tradition. Not only does it challenge my beliefs on a daily basis but it reminds me of the great gifts and strengths lying in other faith traditions. The more absurd and arcane ways of Friends quickly crumble under the scrutiny of Roger's ecumenical stance. His refusal to sign up to any one denomination but to attend services of several, can cause misunderstanding as sometimes they think they have captured him and then he slips away! However, if he were committed to one church and therefore as involved as I am in the day to day support of his congregation things might be more complicated and we are aware of couples where this is so. I joined Friends because I was looking for a faith group where gender was not an issue. I had had enough of fighting the "women in ministry" corner. I did not feel what so many Friends describe as "coming home", just that I had joined a group of people around whom I felt comfortable and with whom I could make a contribution to things I cared about. The issues around a Quaker married to a non-Quaker are not just about time and money but also where heart, soul and spirit reside. Having taken a different path to that of my partner, we have two such "homes" and it requires openness, effort and imagination to keep the paths clear, the gates open and to share the beauties of each other's home and garden.

Perhaps one of the dangers for Quakers is that we tend only to talk to ourselves. At a Woodbrooke development weekend we worked with the Myers-Briggs Type Indicator and nearly everyone fell into a very narrow range of types. Some types were not represented at all. We need to hear the sometimes abrasive voice of those who are not similar to us. I hear that every day. What we do together is more important than whether we recite the same creed.

𝔖 *Roger writes . . .*

The concerns associated with single Quakers in families are not confined to the Religious Society of Friends. The Association of Interchurch Families, founded in 1967 (see Resources list p.111), is a support network for families in which the partners belong to different denominations. It is mainly involved with Roman Catholics married to those of other denominations but all interchurch families are made welcome, and the problems are often similar, whatever the denomination.

I understand the responsibilities of being a member of a religious organisation which has no local paid staff and I have been happy to have been alongside Susan as she has gradually become increasingly involved with Friends activities, both locally and nationally. I have certainly benefited from this association and am grateful to Friends for introducing me to concepts such as Bible sharing and aspects of the Quaker non-voting "business method" which I have been able to pass on to other organisations right outside the Quaker orbit. I do what I can to support her in her Quaker involvement and I do not have reason to complain of the time and effort which she contributes. Quite the reverse. I am proud of her association with Friends and mention it, with pride, to friends and acquaintances. I can sit comfortably with the silence of meeting for worship and wish there was more silence in the worship of other denominations. I have joined with Friends in the peace witness at Molesworth and Aldermaston and at the silent prayer vigil which takes place monthly in the town centre of Northampton, under the auspices of the local Christian interdenominational network for justice and peace. I have spent happy months at Woodbrooke. Looking back, I realise that I am an unreconstructed joiner of organisations; I estimate that I have joined over fifty organisations during the years of our marriage, associations, churches, political parties, sports clubs. So it is a fair question to ask why I have not become an attender or a member. There are two reasons.

First, since a conversion experience as a student in 1947, I have believed implicitly that Jesus was not only a historical figure but also was and still is the Messiah whom the Jews had been expecting for many years and for whom orthodox Jews are still waiting. I believe Jesus is part of the Trinity and that his life on earth was the only time in recorded history when God has been incorporated as a human being to show us the way. This incarnational belief is so fundamental to my faith journey that I would find it very difficult to be committed to a religious organisation which does not specifically hold this view, and is divided, some would say unhappily divided, by an ongoing debate about the person of Jesus. Within Quakers, many "universalists" regard the historical Jesus as a significant teacher, wise person, prophet, whereas the "Christocentrics" go a step further and I am with them. Jesus prayed that all believers "may be one" (John 17: 11) and we live in an era when real progress is being made towards Christian unity but, unfortunately, Friends are split on this issue. Although many individual Friends are Christians, the Society itself cannot easily be part of a corporate Christian witness and sometimes has to stand, rather diffidently, on the sidelines. I feel the need to stand uncompromisingly with Christian organisations.

Secondly, I find that my faith is underpinned by sacraments, outward and visible signs with inward and spiritual meanings. I want to believe but I have times of doubt, like many of us, and at these times I need all the support I can find to enhance faith. These supports include prayer, Bible study and, for me, the sacrament of the eucharist, the bread and wine. Friends, of course, do not reject sacraments and even give them pride of place by saying that all life is sacramental:

> We do not judge our fellow Christians to whom the outward sacraments mean so much. Rather do we wish, by prayerful fellowship with them, to be led unitedly with them to a deeper understanding of what underlies those sacraments, and so to share a richer experience of the mind of Christ (*Quaker Faith and Practice* 27.39).

I envy them the idealism of this holistic view but, for me, sacramental occasions are important and not to be avoided. If every day is Christmas, there is no Christmas. If Christ is risen every day, there is no Easter. If everyone is my friend, I have no friends. I unite with the Quaker view that all life is sacramental but not with the corollary that there is no need for specific sacraments, whether it be the steeple pointing to heaven or the bread and wine of the eucharist.

Maybe in the 17th century the steeple had become more important as an architectural masterpiece than a help to the worship of the congregation at its base. Maybe the smells and bells were almost regarded as objects of worship in themselves rather than symbols with spiritual meaning. So the problem was one of idolatry and Fox and his followers saw the need to simplify and minimise the outward and visible in order to maximise the inward and spiritual. If I had been born in 1627 instead of 1927 I might easily have become an early Quaker, but the world has changed and idolatry has changed with it. There is little risk now of the kind of "religious" idolatry that Fox railed against and today we are more likely to worship the washing machine than the church steeple, the internet rather than the incense. The consumerist forces surround us on every side, controlled with ever-increasing refinement by their advocates, trained by psychologists and turned out by business schools which have no truck with a spiritual path, or at most, relegate it to someone else to deal with. And if these sophisticated forces of secularism surround me, nearing eighty with few prospects, how much more they must surround our children in their forties and our teenage grandchildren assimilating values to live by.

The faith community has changed too since Fox's time. Early Quakers and all others accepted the divinity of Jesus, for example. The problems were about how such belief was to be put into practice rather than the belief itself, but since that era, Christian belief has been assailed for two hundred years by waves of secularists, scientists, humanists, Marxists and others. So those like myself, having a gut feeling that the Gospels are a vital record of God uniquely breaking into our human world, are now in a minority and need all the underpinning we can lay hands on, including sacramental worship and especially the bread and wine of the eucharist. Without such help I would be likely to find myself in a spiritual desert where I do not want to be. I gladly attend meeting for worship from time to time, feel at home with Quakers, find inspiration in the testimonies, am truly grateful for these gifts and hope to show appreciation in practical ways. But I have never been able to consider myself as an attender nor applied for membership. In the book, Susan (member) is listed as "married to Roger" and she is therefore a "single Quaker in the family" (SQUIF).

There are of course Quakers who are also members of other Christian denominations and there are Quakers who attend eucharistic services. Not long ago at a Roman Catholic mass I noticed two who had arrived independently and were surprised to see each other, and perhaps slightly embarrassed. An article by Peter Varney in *The Friend* (20 May 2005) tentatively proposed that Quakers might embrace some form of eucharist within meeting for worship. This would indeed be a witness to unity and inclusivity and would also draw in those like myself who are close to Friends but do not wish to abandon specific sacraments. Worship occasions such as the eucharist and celebration days such as Christmas and Easter are stepping stones in faith across the river of materialism, hypocrisy, selfishness and downright evil which sometimes threatens to engulf me and those I see around me.

So I am a postmodern interdenominational Christian, worshipping in all manner of churches, involved in a number of ecumenical projects, a longterm active member of The Neighbours Community which stands for Christian unity,* but unlikely to join the Religious Society of Friends. That said, this difference of faith journeys is not a great problem between Susan and myself. We understand one another's situations, with their strengths and weaknesses, and do what we can to support each other in concerns which are so important to us both. And, of course, marriage itself is a sacrament, an outward and visible sign to others and an inward and spiritual resource to ourselves, a pearl of great price.

---

*The Neighbours Community statement of purpose includes the phrase, "Our wider aims are to encourage Christian unity and community and to seek understanding with those of different faiths."

6 To Conclude

Two places stand out as distinctive steps in the journey of our marriage, Hanita in Israel and Amorgos, a Greek island. In 1967 we travelled overland from Sheffield to Jerusalem, a pilgrimage journey of 7,000 miles. We stayed on a kibbutz in northern Galilee, near the border with Lebanon. The inspirational experience of living in community, and working in the self-governing kibbutz engineering business making high speed steel cutting tools, was a major factor in our subsequent decision that Roger should not return to his work as a manager in the steel industry, but should spend what turned out to be the rest of his working life, thirty years, in the counter-cultural field of employee-owned co-operative businesses.

Years later the ideas in this book were often discussed and some of it written at Theologos, a small uninhabited monastery on a remote Greek island, where we have been regular summer visitors since 1992. Theologos is several miles from the nearest habitation and there is no road to it, only a stepped donkey track. Rather than being built on a level foundation, the 9th century monastery appears to have grown out of the ground and its contours follow the irregular outline of the rocky hillside. Some of the seats in the church are the living rock itself, not made with hands, and it has been a place of prayer for over a thousand years, a place of silence. The stepped track has led to the monastery for all of these thousand years and although we have not been married that long, we could say that our marriage has been a stepped path for fifty years. There have been the locational steps of moving house, first from Sheffield where we met and married and where our children were born, to Northampton, abandoning the much-travelled path of conventional industry to develop a different kind of working group, and later, abandoning our outer suburbs detached house in 1984 to initiate The Neighbours Community a mile nearer the town centre.

The vertical height of the steps on the donkey track vary but all are within the capability of the donkey to surmount them. Watching from a distance the donkeys appear to be travelling smoothly uphill, taking the steps in their stride in a seemingly effortless progression towards their destination. We ponder the analogy and are not at all sure that we can say the same.

Theologos Monastery

There is a further correspondence. Although Theologos is remote and uninhabited, there are goats to be watered and even a patch of vines to be nurtured in a sheltered fold of the hills. So the path is used by donkeys every day, from the nearest village. Broken steps are repaired, overhanging branches trimmed. Although our marriage is a long one, we are aware that it cannot be taken for granted and if there are broken places, they need to be repaired. If the path is to continue, we need to look ahead with vision as well as looking back with thankfulness for gifts received.

In the latter half of the 20th century it became apparent that Theologos needed urgent restoration or it would become a roofless ruin. A local monk has the vision to see it becoming a "working monastery" again and has overseen the restorative work. Initially he was almost alone in this task but now he is supported by local people and even by a few visitors like ourselves.

The purpose of the building, to be a witness to the presence of God, is unchanged over a thousand years but the way it will be used in this century will undoubtedly be different from previous centuries and it is here that vision is needed.

Correspondingly for marriage. The modernist certainties of the enlightenment of the last two centuries are now gradually giving way to the postmodernist unknowing uncertainties. Many people are rejecting dogma and some are also rejecting statements of common purpose so there is a hesitation to join a religious organisation, or a political party or even a stamp collecting club for fear there is an awful commitment to collect only foreign stamps or to reject modernist self-adhesive ones. Such postmodernism affects relationships so that there is a tendency to adopt the cautious option of living together "for as long as we choose" rather than taking the commitment step to marry for life. The positive result of this is to diminish the risk of being trapped in an unhappy, unloving, lifelong marriage, but the corresponding negative result is to lose the synergy of a lifelong committed relationship. The synergetic baby may be thrown out with the bathwater.

Quakers, with their carefully tended aversion to dogma, are in a stronger position than most religious organisations to benefit from postmodernism but, believing in the value of longterm relationships and the spirituality of the long haul, perhaps they need to think out how such relationships are initiated and nurtured. A Friend, soon to be married, searches in vain for a marriage preparation course within her faith tradition.

There is no more important phrase in marriage than the simple "I love you", with the implication that because I love you, ours is a committed longterm relationship which will change our lives, and we accept these changes, "for better for worse, for richer for poorer."

The building up of the good society, identified for Quakers by the testimonies of peace, integrity, equality, simplicity, community, is a long haul operation requiring perseverance in the face of

inevitable setbacks. Our conclusion is that the synergy of marriage
will contribute more than the intermittent energy resulting from less
committed relationships.

"What canst thou say?" We were asked to write about our long
marriage especially because our spiritual journeys have diverged,
Susan towards Quakerism and Roger towards interdenominational
Christianity. We have tried to recognise each other's boundaries and
affirm each other's callings. The synergy thus generated has enabled us
to adopt an unconventional upside down lifestyle, community living
rather than a separate household, co-operative working rather than
"external" ownership. However, the task of re-envisioning marriage in
the postmodernist world is not for us to work out at threescore years
and more but for younger people. The best we can do is to affirm and
encourage them and we gladly set our gnarled hands to this task.

Appendix A

1975: Community Living in Weston Favell – an aunt sally

Some Random Thoughts on a Cell House

The reason for considering a cell house is that it may help us (= a group of committed Christians = body of Christ = church) to adopt a lifestyle to which we aspire but cannot easily make effective when living in five separated houses. Outward and visible signs of such a lifestyle might be:

1. more regular prayer/eucharist/meeting/eating together
2. more effective caring and sharing of babysitting, cars, grannysitting, lawn mowers, visitors, food buying
3. possibility of some cell members working together on some commercial project (wholesale food shop, light industry, café/meeting place) or some therapeutic project (providing home for nervous breakdown, aged, mentally handicapped)

What Sort of Building?

Assuming we stay in Northampton, the cell house might consist of several separate but interconnected family houses in one building. Five families would need a total of at least 20 bedrooms, 10 living rooms, etc. Flexibility would be needed to accommodate longstay relatives (= widowed mother or abandoned cousin) and short stay visitors and neighbours. Large rooms such as barns, workshops, outhouses would provide for 3. above. These requirements indicate either a purpose-designed building (expensive? good ambience? difficult planning permission?) or an existing hotel or hostel (too institutional? not many available?) or a row of old or new terrace houses or courtyard (difficult to buy whole row with vacant possession?)

Where?

An area where planning permission for integrated living and working is possible (eg not a trading estate nor an exclusive residential area?).

How Much?

For a minimum scheme local terrace houses sell for £5,000–£8,000 and conversion cost might be £3,000–£5,000. So a group of six houses would cost minimum £48,000. A realistic estimate might be between £50,000 and £100,000? Figures of this order are unlikely to be beyond our scope and a Housing Association might be the best vehicle. The style would be frugal comfort.

When?

If cell families agreed in principle, it would not be necessary for all to move in from the start, or ever. It would be necessary for, say, one or two families to be prepared to move whenever the right place was ready.

Roger Sawtell, 3.11.75

Appendix B

The Neighbours Community, Northampton

Founded in 1984, we are a community of households. Fifteen people, some single, some married, some children. Each household lives in one of five adjacent terrace houses, with a common meeting room and a large garden. We are ecumenical Christians (Anglican, Quaker, Catholic), pray together every morning and share some meals each week. Our stated purpose is "to develop a community life which enables us to explore and share our faith and care for others according to the Gospel". Our wider aims are to encourage Christian unity and community and to seek understanding with those of other faiths. We arrange creativity mornings and quiet days and offer hospitality to visiting groups. We have a contemplative eucharist each month and a Taizé prayer. We lead diverse lives, some in paid work, some voluntary. We try to support each other, and visiting friends, in our different journeys and callings.

May 2005

Appendix C

An Agapé based on Matthew 26:26–28

A piece of homemade bread and a cup of wine are placed on the table. Before the meal, the leader says:

This is the bread, not bought from a shop, but lovingly made in our kitchen, full of seeds and risen with fresh yeast.

This is "bread", a symbol of our material prosperity, which is not so much of our making but due to happenstance and by grace, the unmerited favour of a loving God.

This is the bread which is broken as we sometimes feel broken, wounded, inadequate, defeated by circumstances.

This is the bread which is a symbol of our life together as a community. We share the same loaf, we are committed to nourish each other.

This is the bread, given for us, which Jesus tells us to eat together, to remind us of his life, death and resurrection. So, let us eat this bread, in silence.

Each breaks off a piece of the bread and gives it to his/her neighbour.

* * *

After the meal the leader says:

This is the wine, poured out for us by Jesus, for forgiveness. As we drink from this cup, let us forgive one another and all who seek forgiveness.

The cup is passed round for each person to drink, in silence.

* * *

All say together:

The grace of our Lord Jesus Christ, and the love of God, and the fellowship of the Holy Spirit be with us all evermore. Amen.

Appendix D

Daily Bread Co-operative Ltd: An Interview

Daily Bread Co-operative is an employee-owned co-operative business in Northampton, packing and selling a wide range of wholefoods. There are thirty four people on the payroll and turnover is £1.5 million. Trading started in 1980 so 2005 is the jubilee year. It is an "upside down" business as the profits are mostly given away, the manager is paid the same as the cleaner, both have one vote, and part of the working day is spent in prayer. Roger Sawtell was a founding member.

Q. *How did Daily Bread start?*
A. As part of my work in 1976 I had put together a set of Model Rules for an employee-owned business. To test the procedure for registering as a co-operative society with social objects rather than an incorporated company, I asked a group of friends to become members of a hypothetical co-operative. Then we decided that perhaps it could be a real business rather than just a testbed.
Q. *So did you make bread?*
A. My task was to find a product and a building. I worked for a few days at a local bakery to get firsthand knowledge and decided that baking was not viable for the business we had in mind. I consulted friends. Bernard said, "Don't go into food. It's too competitive." I looked at furniture refurbishment, or bicycle maintenance and eventually proposed wholefood. So we went into food. John said, "Don't start now, there's a recession." But we needed to start to fulfil one of the objects, to provide supportive work for people recovering from mental illness. Liz said, "Don't put your house up for security, you may lose it." So we didn't. George said, "Wait for a Labour Government. The Tories will kill you off." We didn't wait and the

Labour Government did not arrive until 1997, seventeen years later! We opened on 1 October 1980, breaking bulk and packing wholefoods for re-sale.

Q. *What were your first products?*

A. We bought a tank with a heated water-jacket, for running-out honey and yeast extract from bulk into jars. We decided to start by offering just these two products to retailers but soon discovered that there was a niche for these and all kinds of other wholefood products for direct sale to the public. There are 3,000 products now.

Q. *Who was the "we"?*

A. A small group of volunteers helped to prepare the building. I became the first employee, shortly followed by Anne Jones and Bill Mills. We grew slowly and steadily with minimal advertising and minimal capital expenditure. Lorries from our suppliers were unloaded by hand. We carried countless sacks on our backs and boxes on hand trolleys.

Q. *Why this "forced manual labour"? There were plenty of mechanical aids, like forklift trucks, available in 1980.*

A. I knew that three out of five new businesses failed during the first two years. We wanted to keep capital expenditure to a minimum to assist survival. Working together as a co-operative group gave us a sense of common purpose. We paid ourselves the same basic wage so there were no disputes about who did what. We set out our principles in what we called the Preamble which has remained unchanged for over twenty years. We repaid the starting loan within the first few years and the business has been self-financing ever since.

Q. *So you survived the vital first two years?*

A. Yes. I soon realised that in a strange upside down manner, all my previous experience in industry had been an unknown preparation for these early years at Daily Bread. It was a deliberately unconventional business but like any business, it had to survive in the market place. Every morning at prayers, we prayed, not for "success" but for discernment to see the way forward in terms of people. E.F. Schumacher's book title was often in my mind, *Small is Beautiful: economics as if people mattered.*

Q. *Prayers? Is that part of the business?*

A. Yes. Daily Bread is a group of Christians and the name comes from the Lord's Prayer. St. Benedict taught that the prayer is the work. There has always been a corporate daily meeting for prayer as part of the working day. Someone calculated that this has caused the "loss" of 40,000 working hours. I think it has not been a "loss" but a significant "gain".

Q. *What is your role now, in 2005?*

A. I stood down as elected manager in 1987, after seven years, and continued as a part-time packer until 1996. Now I'm a regular visitor and customer but have had no formal role in the co-operative for a good many years. Just as well, I think, as sometimes founders can overstay their usefulness!

Q. *How do you see the business now?*

A. It has adapted and matured like any healthy organism. It is more secure. The present working group is over thirty people and they are wonderful. I know pride is a sin but I can't help being proud of them. I believe the 21st century will see a huge increase in co-operative working. The Daily Bread experience could be useful for many future employee-owned co-operative businesses.

Daily Bread Co-operative Ltd. The Old Laundry, Bedford Road, Northampton NN4 7AD.
01604 621531
northampton@dailybread.co.uk
www.dailybread.co.uk

John Kerr, a working member of Daily Bread Co-operative, has written an anecdotal account, *25 Years Already? Crumbs!* Available from the above address.

For information about co-operatives:
Co-operatives UK, Holyoake House, Hanover Street, Manchester M60 0AS.
01612 462900
pgreen.coopunion@co-op.uk
www.cooperatives-uk.coop

Publications referred to in this book

Books

Benedict. *The Rule of Saint Benedict*, translated by Abbot Parry. Leominster: Gracewing, 1990, ISBN 0852441681

Bloy, Philip. *The Call to Mission Answered*. Ann Arbor, MI: Disciples Press, 2000, ISBN 0 946 46510 9

Braithwaite, W.C. *The Beginnings of Quakerism*. Macmillan, 1923; 2nd ed Cambridge University Press, 1955; repr York: Sessions ISBN 0 900657 25 1

Brown, Peter. *The Body and Society: Men, Women and Sexual Renunciation in Early Christianity*. Faber & Faber, 1988, ISBN 0 571 14398 9

Buber, Martin. *Between Man and Man*. Routledge, 1947, ISBN 0 415 27827 9

Chittister, Joan. *The Rule of St.Benedict*. St Paul's, 1992, ISBN 0854394281

Coleman, Peter. *Christian Attitudes to Marriage*. SCM Press, 2004, ISBN 0 334 02956 2

de Waal, Esther. *Seeking God*. Fount Paperbacks 1984 ISBN 0 00 626687 8

Diggers and Dreamers: the guide to communal living 2004/2005. D&D Publications, 2004, ISBN 0 954 5757 0 9

Fiorenza, Elizabeth S. *In Memory of Her*. SCM, 1983, ISBN 0 334 02081 6

Fromm, Eric. *The Art of Loving*. George Allen and Unwin, 1957, repr Thorsons, 1995, ISBN 1 85538 505 8

Funk, Robert, et al. *The Five Gospels. The Search for the Authentic Words of Jesus*. HarperCollins, 1997, ISBN 0 02 541949 8

Gardiner, Patrick. *Kierkegaard: A Very Short Introduction*. Oxford: OUP, 2002, ISBN 0 19 280256 9

Gibran, Khalil. *The Prophet*. Pan Books, 1991, ISBN 0 330 31972 8

Grey, Mary. *Prophecy and Mysticism*. Edinburgh: T & T Clark, 1997, ISBN 0567085872

Griswold, Robert. *Creeds and Quakers*. Wallington, PA: Pendle Hill, 2005 (Pendle Hill Pamphlet 377), ISBN 0 87574 377 3

Hatton, Jean. *Betsy: The dramatic biography of a prison reformer*. Crowborough: Monarch Books, 2005, ISBN 1 85424 705 0

Hayden, Judith. *In Search of Margaret Fell*. Quaker Books, 2002, ISBN 0 85245 335 3

Horle, Craig W. *Quakers and the English Legal System*. Philadelphia, PA: University of Pennsylvania Press, 1988, ISBN 0 8122 8101 2

Jones, Rufus. *The Later Periods of Quakerism*. Macmillan, 1921

Jung, Carl. "The Love Problems of Students", lecture at University of Zurich 1924, in *Analytical Psychology*. Kegan Paul, 1928

Kerr, John. *25 Years Already? Crumbs!* Northampton: Daily Bread Co-operative, 2005

The Little Gidding Prayer Book. SPCK, 1986, ISBN 0281042438

May, Rollo. *Love and Will*. Fontana, 1972, ISBN 0006428452

McGrandle, P. *Trevor Huddleston: Turbulent Priest*. Continuum, 2004 ISBN 0 8264 7123 4 (Afterword by Rowan Williams).

Moore, Thomas. *Dark Nights of the Soul*. Piatkus Books, 2004, ISBN 0 7499 2557 4

Myers, Isabel. *Gifts Differing*. Palo Alto, CA: Davies-Black, 1980, ISBN 0 89106 074 X

O'Shea, Ursula Jane. *Living The Way: Quaker Spirituality and Community*. Quaker Books, 2003, ISBN 0 85245 348 5. First published by Margaret Fell Quaker Publishers (Australia), 1993 ISBN 0 909885 35 4

Quaker Faith and Practice (QFP): The book of Christian discipline of the Yearly Meeting of the Religious Society of Friends (Quakers) in Britain. Britain Yearly Meeting, 1995; 3rd edn, 2005, ISBN 0 85245 375 2

Sawtell, Mary. *Lives on Hold: Homeless Families*. Maternity Alliance 2002, ISBN 0 946741 75 1

Sawtell, Roger. *Sharing Our Industrial Future*. Edgbaston: The Industrial Society, 1968, ISBN 0852900082

Schumacher, E.F. *Small is Beautiful: economics as if people mattered*. Blond and Briggs, 1973, ISBN 085634012X

A Simple Communion: arranged for house meetings. Northampton: Daily Bread Co-operative, 1980

Storr, Anthony. *Jung*. Fontana, 1973, ISBN 0006860311

Trevett, Christine. *Women in Quakerism in the 17th.Century*. York: Sessions, 1991 ISBN 1 85072 087 8

Tyler, Anne. *A Patchwork Planet*. Vintage, 1999, ISBN 0 09 927268 7

Wallis, Jack. *Jung and the Quaker Way.* QHS, 1988; 2nd edn Quaker
   Home Service, 1999, ISBN 0 85245 310 8
Vanier, Jean. *Community and Growth.* Darton Longman & Todd, 1989
   (2nd edn), ISBN 0 232 51814 9
Yoder, John Howard. *The Original Revolution.* Scottdale, PA: Herald
   Press, 1971. Extract cited here found also in *Watch for the
   Light.* Farmington, PA: The Plough Publishing House, 2001,
   ISBN 0 874869 17 X

Articles

"Nothing is sacred in love and bank statements" *The Guardian,* 5 April
   2005
Riddell, Mary. "See you in court". *New Statesman,* 29 November 2004
Peter Varney, "Friends and the Eucharist". *The Friend,* 20 May 2005

Further Reading

Bieber, Nancy. *Communion for a Quaker.* Wallingford, PA: Pendle Hill Publications, 1997, ISBN 0875743315

Boulding, Elise. *One Small Plot of Heaven: Reflections on Family Life by a Quaker Sociologist.* Wallingford, PA: Pendle Hill Publications, 1986, ISBN 0875749127

Boulding, Kenneth. *Sonnets on Courtship, Marriage and Family.* Wallingford, PA: Pendle Hill Publications, ISBN 093600102X

Committee on Eldership and Oversight (Britain Yearly Meeting). *Committed Relationships.* Quaker Books, 2001. ISBN 0 85245 330 2

Committee on Eldership and Oversight (Britain Yearly Meeting). *This is Who I am: Listening with Older Friends.* Quaker Books, 2004, ISBN 0 85245 351 5

Divorce & changing family patterns project of Children & Young People's Committee (Britain Yearly Meeting); ed. Fiona Burtt. *When the Wind Changes: Young people's experiences of divorce and changing family patterns.* Quaker Home Service, 2001

Family Life Sub-Committee (New England Yearly Meeting). *Living with Oneself and Others.* Worcester, MA: New England YM, Committee on Ministry and Counsel, 1993

Family Relations Committee (New England Yearly Meeting). *A Quaker Marriage: In the Presence of God.* Philadelphia, PA: Philadelphia Yearly Meeting, 1988

Family Relations Committee (Philadelphia Yearly Meeting). *Resource Guide to be Used by Same-Sex Couples.* Philadelphia, PA: Philadelphia Yearly Meeting, 1991

Farnham, Suzanne, et al. *Listening Hearts: Discerning Call in Community.* Harrisburg, PA: Morehouse Publishing, 1991, ISBN 0819215635

Hill, Leslie. *Marriage: A Spiritual Leading for Lesbian, Gay and Straight Couples.* Wallingford, PA: Pendle Hill Publications, 1993, ISBN 0875743080

McBee, Patricia (ed.). *Grounded in God: Care and Nurture in Friends Meetings.* Philadelphia, PA: Quaker Press of Friends General Conference, 2002, ISBN 1 88830 571 1

Milligan, Edward. *Quaker Marriage.* Kendal: Quaker Tapestry Scheme, 1994, ISBN 0951158163

O'Shea, Ursula Jane. *Living the Way: Quaker Spirituality and Community.* Quaker Books, 2003, ISBN 0852453485

Quaker Lesbian and Gay Fellowship. *Speaking our Truth: Plain Quaker's guide to lesbian and gay lives.* 1993

Rehard, Mary Kay. *Bringing God Home: Family Spirituality.* Wallingford, PA: Pendle Hill Publications

Watson, Elizabeth. *Marriage in the Light: Reflections on Marriage and the Clearness Process.* Philadelphia, PA: Philadelphia Yearly Meeting, 1993, ASIN B0006QE1UI

Whitmire, Catherine. *Plain Living: A Quaker Path to Simplicity.* Notre Dame, IN: Sorin Books (Ave Maria Press), 2001, ISBN 1893732282

Resources

Marriage and relationships

Association of Interchurch Families
Bastille Court, 2 Paris Garden, London SE1 8ND
telephone: 020 7651 7254
e-mail: info@interchurchfamilies.org.uk
website: www.interchurchfamilies.org.uk

Relate
Relate Central Office, Herbert Gray College, Little Church Street,
Rugby, Warwickshire, CV21 3AP
telephone: (lo-call) 0845 456 1310 or 01788 573241
website: www.relate.org.uk

Religious communities etc

Benedictines
website: www.benedictines.org.uk

The Iona Community
Savoy House, 140 Sauchiehall St, Glasgow, Scotland, G2 3DH
telephone: 0141 332 6343
fax: 0141 332 1090
e-mail: ionacomm@gla.iona.org.uk
website: www.iona.org.uk

Co-operatives

Co-operatives UK
Holyoake House, Hanover Street, Manchester M60 0AS
telephone: 01612 462900
e-mail: pgreen.coopunion@co-op.uk
website: www.cooperatives-uk.coop

Diggers and Dreamers
c/o Edge of Time Ltd, BCM Edge, London, WC1N 3XX
e-mail: info@diggersanddreamers.org.uk
website: www.diggersanddreamers.org.uk